# JOHNNY OTIS

## RED BEANS & RICE
### and other Rock 'n' Roll Recipes

POMEGRANATE ARTBOOKS ■ SAN FRANCISCO

Published by Pomegranate
Box 6099, Rohnert Park, CA 94927

Pomegranate Europe Ltd.
Fullbridge House, Fullbridge
Maldon, Essex CM9 7LE, England

Pomegranate Catalog No. A902

**Library of Congress Cataloging-in-Publication Data**

Otis, Johnny. 1921–
        Red beans & rice and other rock 'n' roll recipes  /  Johhny Otis. —
1st ed.
                p.     cm.
        Includes index.
        ISBN 0-7649-0361-6
        1. Cookery, American.     2. Cookery, International.     I. Title.
TX715.083     1997
641.5973—dc21                                              97-17359
                                                                            CIP

Designed by Riba Taylor

Printed in Canada
06  05  04  03  02  01  00  99  98  97
10  9  8  7  6  5  4  3  2  1
First Edition

# CONTENTS

# INTRODUCTION

It seems that so much of what I have known and enjoyed about my friends over the years has had to do with what they like to cook and eat, and what we have liked to cook and eat together. My family has always been big on cooking, and I even owned a deli for a while. So I've been collecting these recipes from a lot of different folks and making up my own for a long time. When I see them all together here, they are almost like a scrapbook of pictures, offering up lots of memories of some great times.

Some of my friends have passed on, and I feel a real loss from not having their contributions to this book. But I have such warm memories of them—I figure they can be part of the book through these few stories.

I ran into Sam Cooke at Elihu "Black Dot" McGee's Bar-B-Q Cafe on Western Avenue in Los Angeles, just after he had left the Soul Stirrers gospel group to pursue a career in popular music. We were enjoying some of Dot's famous ribs, and Sam, whom I had met earlier, was telling me of his plans to try his hand at making some rhythm and blues records. He did try, of course, and his first attempt resulted in the sensational hit "You Send Me," which remains a big favorite to this day.

Black Dot had originally been the owner of an illegal horse-betting establishment on Central Avenue. He was a very popular guy with a nice personality. Everyone liked Black Dot, even the police, and of course, they had good reason to because Dot—like other bookies, after-hours spot proprietors, and various hustlers—had to grease the cops' palms to stay in business.

By the time Sam Cooke and I met at Dot's barbecue joint, Elihu had a long since left horse booking and had become a legitimate restaurant owner.

The few times Sam had dinner at our house I remember he ate like a bird. He used to compliment Phyllis on her spaghetti, but he never ate a lot.

Johnny Otis and Sam Cooke, 1957

Johnny Otis and Willa Mae "Big Mama" Thornton at the Apollo Theatre in Harlem, New York, 1954

Johnny Otis and Little Willie John, c. 1953

I found Big Mama Thornton in Houston in 1954. Even back then, there was no doubt in any knowledgeable person's mind: she was a *great* blues singer. As soon as she strode out on the stage smiling, the audience reacted. There was more to her than a big, charismatic presence, however. She could just flat out *sing*. I'm really sorry that Big Mama didn't live to enjoy the present day blues fad. She would have been the undisputed queen.

She and I had an affectionate friendship. We were pals in the true sense of the word. One night, a drunk at a dance in Lake Wales, Florida, slapped me. No reason, just POW! Before I could get myself together, Big Mama had mopped up the floor with him—and this was a big dude! "Don't *nobody* mess with my buddy!" she shouted.

Big Mama went for soul food dishes in a big way. Sometimes I'd lay some smothered steak and collards on her, and other times she'd cook us a pot of oxtail stew and rice—always delicious.

I found Little Willie John on a talent show in Detroit in 1951. By the time this photo was taken, Willie John was a big star. His hit records included "Fever," "All Around the World," and "I Need Your Love So Bad."

For such a little guy, he had a humongous appetite. He always seemed to show up just at dinner time. My drummer Kansas City Bell used to call out, "Hide the neck bones quick! Here comes Little Willie John!"

Willie John would have approved of the neck bones recipe on page 2.

Johnny Otis and
Dizzy Gillespie

One day back in the fifties I was having lunch
in a little café in Atlanta along with Dizzy
Gillespie, Big Mama Thornton, and Little Willie
John. Willie John had declared that week that he
was going to become vegetarian. Big Mama and I
had oxtails. We tasted them, and they were so
good we went back to the kitchen to pick the
chef's brain. When we got back to the table, my
oxtails had been decimated. I was sure Diz hadn't
devoured my food, so I turned to Willie John,
who was trying to look so innocent, and said, "I
thought you were such a big vegetarian, sucker!"
Diz and Big Mama almost choked laughing.

I really enjoyed test-cooking all the recipes in this
book. I hope you do, too.

# JOHNNY'S FAVORITES

As I reviewed for use in this cookbook the recipes I've collected over the years, I was reminded of how many friends, family members, and fellow musicians had contributed to the list. For example, Count Basie's late great drummer, Jo Jones. One day in the 1970s, at his daughter's home in southern California, Jo was giving me a lesson in how to prepare red beans and rice and how to present an R&B musical revue; both subjects were dealt with simultaneously in his typically rapid-fire delivery style, and it was left to me to try to follow his advice as he jumped from beans to boogie. Red beans, Jo explained, can be delicious many ways, but none is better than simply boiled with salt and pepper, ham hocks, chopped garlic, bay leaves, and a pinch of cayenne pepper. The meal he came up with that day made his point eloquently. When presenting a musical show, Jo's idea was to hit 'em with everything you've got in the first number; that way, you're way ahead of the game. So I'm going to apply Jo's show business theory to the opening recipes in this book.

My favorite dishes are pastas. I love 'em all. Hardly a day passes that I don't enjoy a pasta dish, usually spaghetti. Next in line is chicken soup—almost any ethnic chicken soup: Jewish Matzo Ball Chicken Soup, Greek Egg and Lemon Chicken Soup, any of the Chinese and Japanese chicken noodle soup varieties, and plain ol' American Chicken Noodle Soup. Let's face it, you can hardly make a bad pot of chicken soup.

However, when my mouth waters for heavy-weight (politically incorrect) dishes, the following three concoctions top my list: Neck Bones and Beans, Oxtail Stew, and Red Beans and Rice—which are southern soul-food–style goodies that should be partaken of with discretion. In other words, because of their high fat content, eaten too regularly they are not good for you—but they sure are good to you!

The Neck Bones and Beans recipe comes down to us from the late Mexie Love through her bandleader/saxophonist son, Preston Love, who is a longtime good friend and a master amateur chef.

I've been whippin' up Oxtail Stew for so long, I don't remember where I learned to cook it, but the Red Beans and Rice dish is à la Papa Jo Jones.

### Neck Bones and Beans

1½ pounds navy beans (Great Northern beans)
4 pork neck bones
1 large onion, chopped
4 cloves garlic, chopped
1 teaspoon sugar
Salt and black pepper to taste
⅛ teaspoon cayenne pepper

Combine ingredients in a large stewpot. Cover with water and cook over medium heat until beans are done. Add water when necessary to avoid scorching.

Serve with white rice and corn bread.

## Oxtail Stew

Dredge eight large pieces of oxtail in flour and brown in a large skillet. Transfer oxtails to a large stewing pot. Add 3 chopped garlic cloves, salt and black pepper to taste, and a pinch or two of cayenne pepper. Cover with water and cook over medium heat for at least 2 hours or until the meat is falling off the bones. Add water when necessary to avoid scorching.

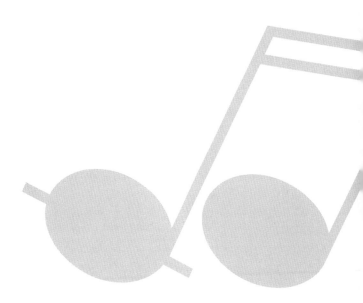

## Red Beans and Rice

Nowadays, interest in Creole and Cajun cooking is at an all-time high. Every August, I produce a Red Beans and Rice Family Music Festival in both southern and northern California. The Southern California edition is spearheaded by Los Angeles County Supervisor Mike Antonovich. The Sonoma County event is held at the Luther Burbank Center for the Arts in Santa Rosa. There are so many delicious versions of Red Beans and Rice entered in our annual cook-offs, I'm glad I'm too busy with the music end of the festival to be involved in the judging.

Every year we see hot, medium, mild, vegetarian, spiced, and unspiced versions, and versions with ham hocks, hot link sausage, chicken, turkey, shrimp, and every combination imaginable. All the dishes have two things in common: red beans and white rice. The variations seem endless, and they are all good because, let's face it, you can't make a bad pot of red beans no matter how you embellish them.

Traveling with my band through the years, I've been able to sample red beans and rice all over the Deep South, including Mississippi, Texas, Georgia, and Alabama, and especially Louisiana, where the African American people of transplanted French culture created the sensational Creole cuisine that is so popular today.

The following recipe is based on the traditional dish as it is served in many black and white homes in the Deep South. It is hearty, unpretentious, and delicious, and it is my favorite way to prepare red beans and rice.

3 ham hocks
1 pound red kidney beans
3 cloves garlic, chopped
3 bay leaves
1 teaspoon salt
⅓ teaspoon black pepper
⅓ teaspoon crushed red pepper or cayenne pepper

In a separate pot, boil the ham hocks for 1 hour.

Combine remaining ingredients in a big pot, cover with water, and bring to a boil. Add the ham hocks to the big pot, and cook over high heat to avoid mushiness. (Simmering over low heat can create a fermenting action, which is to be avoided.) Stir frequently, and keep adding water when needed to avoid sticking and burning.

When the beans are well done, the dish is ready to serve. I usually let the pot cool and put it in the refrigerator overnight. Cooling overnight seems to improve the texture.

Serve over white rice.

Have a bottle of Louisiana Hot Sauce available for those who like it hot.

### Deviled Eggs

Boil 12 eggs for 15 minutes. Cool off immediately by putting eggs in strainer and rinsing with cool water. Take off shells and place eggs in cooler. When eggs are cooled off, cut in half the long way. With small spoon, take out yokes. Mash yokes with ¼ cup of mayo or less. Add a little bit of salt and pepper to taste. Spoon back into egg whites. Sprinkle a little dash of paprika for color, and they are done.

**Note:** For a spicier version, add ⅓ medium onion, finely minced, and ¼ teaspoon cayenne pepper.

## ETTA JAMES

In 1954, I discovered a sensational 16-year-old girl singer in San Francisco. Her name was Jamesetta Rogers. I shortened it to Etta James. I took her to Los Angeles and made her my featured female vocalist. My male vocalist at the time was the fabulous Richard Berry. They made a great singing team, as evidenced by her *Roll with Me Henry/Dance with Me, Henry* smash-hit record. She lived at my house in those days, and I noticed she had a penchant for olives.

One day, after watching her polish off a full can of olives, I asked her, "Hey, baby, how come you love olives so much?" Her answer was, "Here, see if you can eat just one." I almost became a compulsive olive chomper that day. Today, my favorites are large Kalamata olives. Etta probably still goes for the American-style canned type.

If you have access to unprocessed olives, here is how to cure them:

### How to Cure Olives

Ceramic crock (smooth glazed finish)—
    at least 10-gallon size
5 gallons olives
5 gallons water
1 can (about 12 ounces) Red Devil lye

Soak olives in water and lye for 24 hours and drain. Refill with fresh water, and soak for 24 hours more. Repeat the soak, drain, refill process three more times (4 days total).

Store cured olives in refrigerator in an olive oil–vinegar mixture.

**Note:** Once olives are cured, they can be prepared with many combinations of olive oil, vinegar, hot peppers, garlic, celery, basil, oregano, thyme, carrots, onions, etc. When you come up with a particularly delicious batch, please call Etta and me!

Etta James and Johnny Otis

## Johnny Otis's Market/Deli/Cabaret Potato Salad

10 medium-size russet potatoes, unpeeled
1 cup celery, medium diced
1 cup green bell pepper, medium diced
1 cup onion, medium diced
4 hard-boiled eggs, chopped
Salt and black pepper
Mayonnaise

Boil potatoes until fairly soft—not mushy. Leave skins on after boiling potatoes. Cut potatoes to approximately 1½-inch cubes. Combine all ingredients in a large mixing bowl. Add salt, black pepper, and mayonnaise to taste.

## Pesto Pasta Salad

1 cup sundried tomatoes
1 pound seashell pasta
1 tablespoon olive oil
7 ounces pesto
6 ounces feta cheese
1½ cups Greek olives
Pinch of oregano
Pinch of cayenne pepper
Salt and pepper

Rinse tomatoes with water to remove excess oil.

Boil pasta with olive oil. Stir regularly to avoid sticking. Rinse pasta in strainer with cold water. Stir all ingredients in a large bowl and add oregano and cayenne pepper. Season with salt and black pepper to taste.

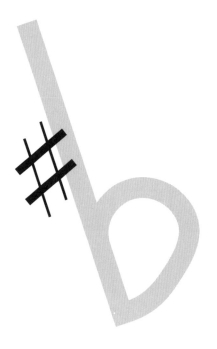

## Tofu Cabbage Salad

We sold a lot of this healthful salad when I had my Deli/Cabaret in Sebastopol.

1 large head of purple cabbage, finely chopped
6 carrots, finely chopped
15 mushrooms, cut in chunks (not thin)
4 scallion stems (about ½ bunch), finely chopped
3 packages tofu (Wildwood brand is good), cut into
    bite-size pieces
3 cloves garlic, finely chopped
2 red bell peppers, finely chopped
1 cup tamari

Mix all ingredients in a large salad bowl with tamari sauce. (Tamari sauce and Teriyaki Tofu by Wildwood are available in most health food stores and increasingly nowadays in supermarkets.)

# GUMBOS, STEWS, CHILI, AND CHOWDER

## Biafran Chicken/Beef Stew

I served this dish to my band members a few years back when we were still living in southern California. The reactions ranged from that of one of my girl singers who said, "Lovely," to a sax player who shouted, "Damn!! This is good. What is it?!!"

½ pound cut-up chuck steak, browned in very hot oil in cast-iron skillet
½ pound cut-up chicken (don't brown)
1 yellow onion, chopped
1 green bell pepper, chopped
1 large can tomatoes
Louisiana Hot Sauce to taste
Salt and black pepper to taste

After beef is browned, put all ingredients in heavy-gauge pot and simmer 1½ hours.
    Serve over rice.

## GUMBO OPTIONS

Everybody who likes to cook seems to have a gumbo recipe. Some are great . . . some not so great. Every one of the gumbo recipes I've included is good. Somewhere here you'll find the one you prefer. I like them all (or they wouldn't be included here), but my personal preference is the gumbo of the common folk of Louisiana. It has no tomatoes, is gray in color, and is usually made with some crab or shrimp. Adding tomatoes, chicken, sausage, oysters, clams, etc., etc. certainly makes a delicious dish, but the gumbo I remember enjoying in friends' homes in New Orleans forty or even fifty years ago was not so glamorous and was quite inexpensive to prepare. I'm talking about poor folks' gumbo. We'd go down to the Mississippi River and visit the Creole farmers and merchants. Or even more fun, we'd go down to the bayous and catch some crab or shrimp.

My ex–son-in-law, Michael Judkins, a Creole of New Orleans origins, explains it this way: "When we move up to California from Louisiana, we make some money and our tastes and attitudes change. We start making glorified gumbo. It's tasty and fine, but I prefer the plain ol' gumbo my Grandma used to make. You know, that gray soup with crab legs in it . . . just pour it over rice, sprinkle some filé and Louisiana Hot Sauce on it, and go for it!!"

Very often in crossword puzzles "gumbo" is given as a clue with "okra" as the answer. Okra is not gumbo!—but it is often added to the dish.

## Cajun Chicken Gumbo

I prefer this dish without tomatoes and with crab, oysters, and clams added.

One 3-pound frying chicken
7 cups water
6 slices bacon, diced
Salad oil
½ cup all-purpose flour
½ teaspoon cayenne pepper
2 large celery stalks, diced
2 medium-size onions, chopped
1 large green bell pepper, chopped
1½ teaspoon salt
1 teaspoon thyme
1 chicken bouillon cube
1 8-ounce can of tomatoes
12 ounces frozen shrimp
1 10-ounce package of frozen, cut okra
3 cups cooked rice, hot

Rinse chicken, with giblets and neck, in cold, running water. Place chicken, breast side down, in 8-quart Dutch oven or saucepan. Add giblets, neck, and water; heat to boiling over high heat. Reduce heat, and simmer for 35 minutes. Transfer chicken, giblets, and neck to large bowl. Refrigerate for 30 minutes. Skim fat from broth in Dutch oven and set aside.

Discard skin and bones. Cut meat and giblets into bite-size pieces.

Brown bacon in small cast-iron skillet over medium-low heat. Remove with slotted spoon to paper towels to drain.

Add salad oil (if necessary) to drippings to bring amount up to ¼ cup. Heat drippings over medium heat until hot. Stir in flour and cayenne pepper; keep cooking and stirring until flour mixture is dark brown but not burned, about 20 minutes. Add celery, onions, and green pepper. Cook until vegetables are tender, stirring often.

Into broth in Dutch oven, stir vegetable mixture, chicken, giblets, bacon, salt, thyme, bouillon, tomatoes (plus liquid), frozen shrimp, and frozen okra. Cook over high heat to boiling. Reduce heat to low and simmer uncovered about 8 minutes, stirring often.

Serve in bowls over rice.

## Chicken Gumbo

A better version of this recipe, in my opinion, replaces the sausage with crab, shrimp, oysters, and clams (or any combination of these seafoods), and eliminates the tomatoes.

2 cups flour
½ pound margarine
1 cup white onions, chopped
1 cup scallions, chopped
8 cloves fresh garlic
2 cups celery, chopped
2 cups bell pepper, chopped
2 quarts chicken stock
2 tablespoons dried thyme
½ teaspoon cayenne pepper
3 bay leaves
Filé seasoning to taste
Salt and pepper to taste
3 pounds fresh okra
4 cups tomatoes (canned or fresh)
2 pounds cooked beef sausage
1 cut-up and boiled chicken (5-pound stewing hen)
Steamed rice

Brown or parch flour in a 400° oven. Stir flour until entire pan is an even nut-brown color.

Melt margarine (reserving 4 tablespoons for okra pot) in a 4-quart pot until very hot. Add flour and stir rapidly, then turn heat down to very low. To the roux, add onions, scallions, garlic, celery, and bell pepper. Keep stirring 'til mixture is a smooth paste.

Pour in chicken stock, add all seasonings, and let mixture come to a boil. Then lower flame and simmer slowly for 40 minutes.

While gumbo pot is simmering, cook okra in margarine in a covered pot for 30 minutes over very low heat. Cook okra 'til it loses its gummy consistency. Then add tomatoes and cook an additional 15 minutes.

Mix contents of both pots together, add cooked sausage and cooked chicken, and allow to simmer for 30 minutes. Serve over steamed rice.

### Roux:

Learning how to concoct a good roux is something you'll need to know if you intend to cook Creole dishes. Sometimes I blow it by being too impatient. When this happens, I have to scrap the project and start all over again. Back in the 1940s, the chef at the old Peavine Club in Reno, Nevada, used to say, "Take it easy, greasy, you got a long way to slide." Good advice in most cooking, and especially when making roux.

2 cups oil
3 cups flour

In a heavy-gauge skillet (preferably cast iron), heat oil gently over low heat. When oil is warm, add flour, mixing as you go. Use a large wooden spoon and keep stirring to keep the flour from burning. Break up any lumps. Keep stirring until the mixture is brownish red. This process can take as long as 25 to 45 minutes. Remember what the old chef said . . . take it easy, greasy, and don't rush it.

After you set the roux aside to cool, be sure to keep stirring occasionally because it will keep cooking until it has cooled down completely.

The cooled roux can be stored in the refrigerator to be used at a later time.

## Chili (I)

4 pounds pork neck bones, cooked down
2 pounds pork hocks (or any pork)
3 tablespoons crushed cumin seed,
    toasted whole and crushed
6 tablespoons chili powder
6 cloves garlic, chopped fine
3 bay leaves, finely crumbled
1 tablespoon salt
$\frac{1}{4}$ teaspoon black pepper
$\frac{1}{4}$ teaspoon cayenne pepper

Put pork in pot with cold water to cover. Bring to a
boil and cook until tender

    Add all the ingredients to the pot, and add water
to cover. Simmer for 45 minutes. Let cool until grease
rises, then skim off fat.

### Toasted Cumin Seeds:

Cook cumin seeds in cast-iron skillet over moderate
heat until lightly toasted. Put cooled seeds between
two layers of heavy wax paper, and crush with a
wooden mallet.

## Chili (II)

Keep a bottle of Habanero hot sauce on the table for those who want their chili blazing hot. A wide choice of Habanero sauce is available from the California Queen of Hot Sauce in Forestville.

(This is not the healthy, vegetarian, low-fat chili I usually concoct. But it just tastes so much better, and once in a great while I just have to make a pot and hope it doesn't kill me!!)

3 pounds chili meat (not regular hamburger meat)
Bacon fat
1 can tomato paste
1 tablespoon cumin seed, toasted and crushed
5 pods garlic, chopped fine
3 tablespoons chili powder
¼ teaspoon cayenne pepper
1 teaspoon salt
¼ teaspoon black pepper

Sauté meat in bacon fat until it changes color from red to gray.

Add tomato paste. Fry until reduced to one-half volume.

Add remaining ingredients—except salt and black pepper—and add water to cover. Simmer for 20 minutes. Add salt and black pepper. Simmer for 10 minutes more.

Serve over rice with or without red beans or kidney beans.

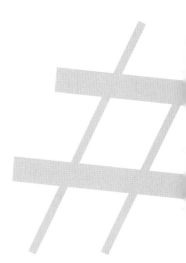

## Fish Chowder

1 3-pound bass-type fish, whole and dressed
3 cups water
Salt
1 teaspoon dried thyme
1 onion, sliced
1 carrot, sliced
2 potatoes, peeled and diced
2 cups milk
2 cups half-and-half
¼ cup butter or margarine, softened
¼ cup flour
Freshly ground black pepper to taste
**Garnishes:** butter, chives

Cut fish fillets into 1-inch cubes. Place head, skin, and bones in a large saucepan with the water. Let simmer about 20 minutes. Strain. To the broth, add the rest of the ingredients, except for the cubed fish. Simmer about 30 minutes or until vegetables are well blended, then add fish cubes and boil for 10 minutes. A touch of cayenne pepper and sweet basil lends an exotic touch to the chowder.

**Note:** For clam chowder, add clams instead of cubed fish at the end.

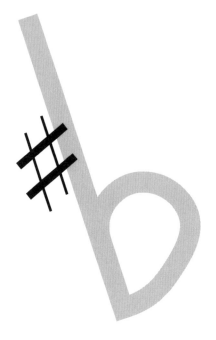

## Vegetarian Chili

Boil 5 cups pinto beans until soft but not mushy, for
1 to 2 hours. Add 1 cup red bell pepper, 1 cup green
bell pepper, and 10 carrots, all cut in thin slices, and
1 package frozen corn. (You can let the corn thaw out
while the beans cook.) Add 1 big can of tomato paste
and 1 big can of tomato sauce. Put on low simmer with
½ cup chili powder, 1 tablespoon of crushed dried chile
peppers, and several garlic cloves, finely chopped.

# OTHER MAIN DISHES

## Chicken Adobo

Back in the 1950s, we played from time to time at a club in San Pedro, California, named The Harlem Hot Spot. We really looked forward to those engagements because at intermission we would eat at a small Filipino restaurant near the club. The old lady who was the chef made the greatest Chicken Adobo I've ever tasted. I remember her son was a man named Ralph who was active politically. I'd love to meet him again and maybe get him on one of my radio or TV shows to tell us about his mom's masterful Chicken Adobo.

½ cup water and ½ cup vinegar per 3-pound
    frying chicken
3 to 6 cloves garlic (to taste)
1 bay leaf, whole
1 teaspoon cracked whole black peppercorns
6 whole peppercorns
½ teaspoon salt
¼ cup soy sauce
¼ teaspoon monosodium glutamate

Marinate all the ingredients together in a large bowl at least 1 hour.

    Simmer in a large, heavy-gauge pot for 45 minutes. Remove chicken when tender. Add water if needed—taste and add water to dilute saltiness. Simmer over low heat while serving.

## Meat Pie

**Pastry (Crust):**

3 cups all-purpose flour

1 teaspoon salt

1 cup shortening

2 eggs

¼ cup plus 1 tablespoon ice water

1 tablespoon vinegar

1 tablespoon milk

**Filling:**

Precooked chicken, beef, or pork

Combine flour and salt; cut in shortening with a pastry blender until mixture is like coarse meal. Combine 1 beaten egg, ice water, and vinegar; sprinkle evenly over surface of meal, and stir with a fork until dry ingredients are moistened.

Shape dough into a ball, divide in two, and roll out. Put one-half on bottom of pie pan, and fill with precooked meat. Put remaining one-half on top.

Beat together remaining egg and 1 tablespoon milk and brush over crust. Puncture crust with fork and bake in a 400° oven for 30 minutes (or until golden brown).

## Sichuan Peanut Sauce for Noodles

2 cups peanut oil
1 heaping cup shelled raw peanuts
½ cup freshly brewed tea, warm
5 garlic cloves
1 tablespoon fresh ginger, coarsely chopped
2 small, fresh green chile peppers
1 teaspoon salt
1 ½ teaspoons sugar
1 tablespoon dark soy sauce
¼ cup fresh lemon juice
2 tablespoons sesame oil
1 tablespoon chili oil
**Garnishes:** coriander and cucumber shreds

Heat peanut oil in wok 'til nearly smoking. Add peanuts, stir gently for 20 seconds. Turn off heat. Let peanuts sit in wok 'til light golden. Use slotted spoon to transfer peanuts from wok to the container of a food processor. Remove all but ¾ cup of the peanut oil.

Grind peanuts to a coarse paste. Add a dash of the tea and the garlic, ginger, and chiles, and continue to blend. Add the remaining peanut oil, and blend briefly. Add the rest of the tea, salt, sugar, soy sauce, and lemon juice, and process to a smooth consistency. Remove to a mixing bowl, and stir in the sesame and chili oils. Mix thoroughly. Serve over egg noodles; garnish with coriander and cucumber shreds.

**Note:** Sauce will keep, refrigerated, for 2 weeks.

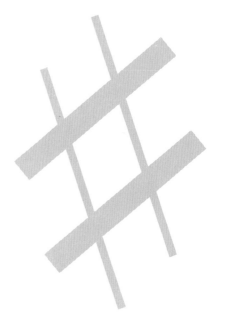

## Senegalese Couscous

5 tablespoons salad oil
6 large chicken thighs
2 onions, sliced
2 cloves fresh garlic, minced
¼ cup all-purpose flour
½ teaspoon cumin
½ teaspoon allspice
¼ teaspoon cayenne pepper
1½ teaspoons turmeric
1 can condensed chicken broth
1 bay leaf
1 pound carrots, sliced
3 red or green bell peppers, cut into 1-inch strips
1 large can garbanzo beans
2 cups couscous (precooked semolina)
¼ cup raisins
1 teaspoon salt
Water

In a 5-quart Dutch oven over medium-high heat, preheat 3 tablespoons salad oil and cook chicken thighs, several at a time, until browned on all sides. Remove them to a plate as they brown.

In drippings remaining in Dutch oven, add onions and garlic and cook until tender, stirring occasionally. Stir in flour, cumin, allspice, cayenne pepper, and 1 teaspoon turmeric until blended; cook 1 minute. Stir in undiluted chicken broth, bay leaf, and 1 cup water; stir while cooking until mixture thickens and boils. Simmer 15 minutes over low heat.

Return chicken thighs to Dutch oven, add carrots and bell peppers, and heat over high heat to boiling. Reduce to low heat, cover tightly, and simmer for 30 minutes. Skim excess fat from liquid, stir in garbanzo beans, and heat through.

Heat 2½ cups water to boiling in a 3-quart saucepan. Stir in couscous, raisins, salt, 2 tablespoons salad oil, and ½ teaspoon turmeric. Remove saucepan from heat; cover and let stand for 5 minutes.

To serve, spoon couscous into center of a large platter. Discard bay leaf from chicken mixture, and spoon chicken thighs and sauce around couscous.

## Tabouli

1 cup dry bulgur wheat, well soaked. (Begin to soak the bulgur at least 3 hours before serving time, and be sure to thoroughly marinate and chill.)

1½ cups boiling water
1½ teaspoons salt
¼ cup fresh lemon or lime juice
1 heaping teaspoon crushed fresh garlic
¼ cup olive oil
½ cup chopped scallions (including greens)
½ teaspoon dried mint
Black pepper to taste
2 medium tomatoes, diced small
1 cup freshly chopped parsley
½ cup coarsely grated carrot
½ cup cooked chickpeas
1 bell pepper, cut into small pieces
1 cucumber, cut into small pieces
1 small summer squash, cut into small pieces
¼ teaspoon dried oregano
**Garnishes:** feta cheese, Greek olives

Combine bulgur, boiling water, and salt in a bowl. Cover and let stand until bulgur is chewable. Rinse in strainer until cooled.

Add lemon juice, garlic, oil, scallions, mint, and black pepper. Mix thoroughly and refrigerate for 2½ hours.

Add vegetables and oregano, and mix gently. Garnish with feta cheese and Greek olives.

### Kenya Dessert—Curried Sweet Potatoes

1 can coconut milk

Brown sugar to taste

1 teaspoon cardamom

3 medium sweet potatoes, cut up

Pour milk, sugar, and cardamom over saucepan of sweet potatoes . . . simmer 'til done.

# RECIPES FROM JOHNNY'S SOULFUL FRIENDS

The recipes that follow here have their roots in all parts of the world. My friends have supplied them with their own commentary—but I can tell you, all of these dishes are delicious!

## BIG BONES

Big Bones plays harmonica and sings the blues beautifully in a deep baritone voice. We appear together from time to time in northern California venues, and I really like what he does on stage. And I like what he does in the kitchen also—check out his "Oh Babe!" Sweet Potato Goody and his Soulful Smothered Steak.

### Chicken and Crab Gumbo

With help from Michelle Lachaux

1 3-pound frying chicken
6 sprigs parsley
1 teaspoon peppercorns
1 bell pepper, chopped
1 large onion, chopped
2 celery stalks with leaves, chopped
2 cloves garlic, chopped
2 carrots, whole
Salt and black pepper to taste
1 cup roux with 1 tablespoon Cajun seasoning mixed in (see roux recipe on page 13)
2 large Dungeness crabs
1 teaspoon filé
**Garnish:** chopped parsley

Boil chicken along with parsley and peppercorns. In a separate pan, sauté bell pepper, onion, celery, and garlic. When meat falls from bones, add two whole carrots and salt. Drain, and separate fat from broth. Discard whole vegetables, chicken skin and bones, return meat to pot, and add sautéed vegetables and roux. Clean crab, and add crab claws. Dissolve filé in 1 cup of the broth, and add to pot. Simmer slowly 15 minutes.

Serve with long-grain rice, and garnish with chopped parsley.

Bones says, "If this Gumbo don't make you almost bite off your fingertips, you've got a problem!"

## "Oh Babe!" Sweet Potato Goody

5 sweet potatoes or garnet yams
¼ pound butter
½ can sweetened condensed milk
3 eggs
½ teaspoon salt
3 tablespoons all-purpose flour
⅓ cup brown sugar
1 teaspoon nutmeg
1 cup raisins
1 cup walnuts
20 large marshmallows

Steam or boil sweet potatoes. Scoop out and retain most of the insides, leaving enough to keep the shells firm. Whip until fine. Add everything but the raisins, marshmallows, and walnuts. Use enough flour to make the filling thick enough to pack into the shells. Stir in nuts and raisins.

Fill shells. Put marshmallows on top of potatoes. Bake in lightly greased pan at 350° for 45 minutes.

## Soulful Smothered Steak

4 pieces cube steak (about 4-by-4 inches each)
3 pats butter
1 onion, sliced whole
10 mushrooms
1 clove garlic
1 regular-size can of mushroom soup
Salt and black pepper
1½ cups water

In butter in a large Dutch oven (with top), sauté meat quickly over high heat. Add onions, mushrooms, and garlic. Cook 'til brown, then add soup, water, salt, and black pepper to taste and cook over medium heat 'til tender.

I serve mashed potatoes with this dish and, always, hot green vegetables. Go for it, but here's a little warning: this smothered steak is so delicious, you must be careful not to bite your fingertips off!

## BILL BOWKER

Bill Bowker is a radio personality and a promoter of musical events in northern California. He got wind of this cookbook and offered the following recipe. I tried it, and I must say—pretty darn good for a blues-loving disc jockey!

### Jumpin' and Jivin' Jambalaya

Serves 8

2 or 3 bay leaves
½ teaspoon each cayenne, white pepper, and black pepper (or to taste)
1 teaspoon salt (or to taste)
1 teaspoon dried thyme and oregano
½ teaspoon sage
3 sausage links, cut into rounds (any type of sausage will do: Polish, kielbasa, sweet Italian, hot links, etc.)
2 cups chicken, cut into bite-size pieces
2 cups onion, chopped
1 cup celery, chopped
1 cup green bell pepper, chopped
1 tablespoon garlic, finely minced
2 cups canned tomatoes, diced, and their juice (when fresh tomatoes are in season, use 2 cups fresh, diced)
½ cup tomato sauce
4 cups chicken stock (or 2 14-ounce cans)
1½ cups long-grain white rice

Mix together seasonings and set aside. Gently cook the sausage and chicken in a little oil about 5 minutes, 'til chicken is no longer pink. Remove from pan and set aside.

Sauté onion and celery in drippings 'til onions are nicely browned. Add bell pepper, garlic, chicken, sausage, and seasoning mix, and cook about 5 minutes. Add the tomatoes with their juice, tomato sauce, and chicken stock, and bring to a boil. Add rice and stir.

Pour into 13-by-9-inch pan, cover with foil, and bake in a 350° oven for 30 minutes. Then remove foil from pan and bake 'til all juices are absorbed and rice is tender (approximately 30 minutes more).

Serve with Spicy Tomato Sauce (see recipe below).

**Note:** If you wish, you may add a pound of de-veined shrimp before you bake the jambalaya. You may also substitute ham for the sausage. When making jambalaya, use whatever you have on hand. It's always delicious!

## Spicy Tomato Sauce

To spoon over Jambalaya

1 32-ounce can chopped tomatoes in tomato juice
1 medium onion, coarsely chopped
1 medium bell pepper, coarsely chopped
2 to 3 stalks of celery, coarsely chopped
1 bay leaf
1 teaspoon each thyme, basil, and oregano
    (or to taste)
½ teaspoon cayenne pepper (or to taste)
1½ teaspoons sugar
2 teaspoons garlic, finely chopped
½ cup tomato sauce
1 cup water

Combine all ingredients in a large skillet. Cook over medium heat approximately 30 minutes, stirring occasionally. Be sure all vegetables are very tender.

## GENE "THE MIGHTY FLEA" CONNERS

Gene Conners (professionally known as "The Mighty Flea") and Big Bones have a few things in common. They are both from the Deep South, both are talented musician/singers, and for the purposes of this book, both are great cooks in the southern soul-food tradition.

I stopped trying to shoot deer long ago, but 30 years back, Flea and I were deer hunting on Sugarloaf Mountain in California. We bagged a large buck, but he fell at the bottom of a ravine. "How are we gonna get him up outta there," I wondered. "Don't worry about it, just help me get him up on my shoulder," Flea said. I still marvel at how he walked up that mountainside with the deer on his back! I saw him do it. He's a small man, but he is powerful. I nicknamed him "The Mighty Flea" on the spot and the moniker stuck. Flea left my show and struck out on his own years ago. He now lives in Germany full time and is very popular with blues/jazz fans throughout Europe.

### Alabama Cracklin' Corn Bread

1½ cups cornmeal
2 cups flour
1 teaspoon salt
½ cup cooking oil
2½ teaspoons baking powder
1 egg, beaten well
1 cup milk
4 slices well-cooked bacon, crumbled into bits

Combine all dry ingredients, then add milk, egg, oil, and bacon bits. Bake in oven at 350° until golden brown.

## Mighty Flea's Chicken Delight

1 large frying chicken
Buttermilk
2 teaspoons salt
2 teaspoons black pepper
1 ½ teaspoons paprika
1 ½ cups yellow cornmeal

Skin chicken and soak overnight in buttermilk.

Put remaining ingredients in a plastic bag and shake well. Add chicken pieces to bag and shake to coat. Place chicken pieces on a rack in a pan.

Bake in preheated oven at 350° until golden brown.

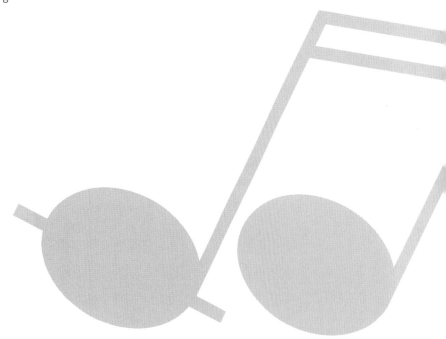

## Quick Chicken and Dumplings

1 large frying chicken, cut into 8 pieces
1 ½ teaspoons salt
2 teaspoons black pepper
¼ teaspoon sage
Pinch of oregano

Fry chicken pieces in heavy-gauge pan for 5 minutes. In a large Dutch oven, combine the remaining ingredients. Add chicken, cover with water, and boil until chicken is tender.

### Dumplings:
(serves 4)
3 cups flour
8 tablespoons oil

Mix flour and oil well and roll out on cutting board. Cut into ½-by-2-inch strips. Drop into pot after chicken has cooked for 15 minutes. Cook until dumplings are done.

## CHRIS COUPER

Chris Couper is one of those people who can do a lot of things and do them all well. He is a cabinetmaker/carpenter, a radio announcer, and a board operator. (He's the board operator for my Saturday morning KPFA radio show.) He's a motorcycle enthusiast and a jazz music lover. In addition, he's also a great cook. During the winter months, we have what we call "Johnny's Soup Kitchen." We broadcast live every Saturday morning from 9:00 to 11:00 a.m. from Copperfield's bookstore in Sebastopol, where we dispense free breakfast pastries, coffee, pizza, and soup. The Village Bakery, the East West Café, and the Slice of Life restaurant supply everything but the soup. Every week, one of my staff—Cam Parry, Dr. George Curtis, Chris Couper, or me—cooks up a giant pot of soup. It has become a contest to see who can concoct the most popular soup.

### Brunswick Stew in Quantity

To many Southerners, Brunswick Stew is made with squirrel meat. But in Polk County, Georgia, where my mother's family is from, it is typically made from a mixture of beef, pork, and chicken, slow-cooked with vegetables and spices. My mother remembers cauldrons of the stuff being prepared at most any civic event, from political rallies to golf tournaments, and the stew was sold by the quart to raise funds for charities. Every local chef had his or her own secret recipe, and open-fire Brunswick Stew cook-offs were commonly held in the community park. My late uncle Jim Berry (a stew chef of some notoriety) recalled that local ministers frequently judged the competitions and that they were present during the entire daylong preparation and cooking process. This was not to provide inspiration, as one might suppose, but rather to claim a share of the moonshine that had been stashed in strategic locations around the park prior to the event. Polk was a dry county, in case you were wondering. Brunswick Stew is only good when made in quantity and it freezes well. Following is Jim Berry's recipe.

4 to 5 pounds pork tenderloin
4 to 5 pounds lean beef rump
4 to 6 whole chicken breasts

Simmer the meats in a large kettle with the following seasonings:

1 tablespoon each salt and pepper
1 bay leaf
1 onion, stuck with cloves

Cook until the meat is falling off the bones. Strain off the broth and add:

3 pounds uncooked lima beans
24 small potatoes
12 onions, chopped
1 cup cut corn
2 cups tomatoes, chopped
1 stalk celery, chopped
1 cup okra, chopped

Cook until vegetables are tender; add meat.
Season with:

1 cup tomato puree
2 cups red wine
1 tablespoon salt
⅛ teaspoon cayenne
1 cup butter
6 tablespoons sugar
3 red chiles
Dash of Tabasco

Cook several hours over low flame.
   Serve with corn bread.

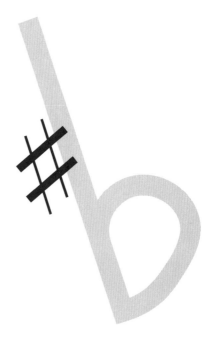

## Curried Fruit

Serves 8

The concept and ingredients may appear strange at first, but this is an OUTSTANDING holiday side dish that really complements turkey, ham, or lamb. One of my most requested recipes. Trust me.

1 12-ounce package mixed dried fruit
   (or mix your own)
1 13-ounce can pineapple chunks
1 21-ounce can cherry pie filling
½ cup dry sherry
¼ cup water
1-2 teaspoons curry powder

Cut large pieces of fruit in half. In 2-quart casserole, combine dried fruit and undrained pineapple. Combine the rest of the ingredients and pour over the fruits. Cover and bake at 350° for 1 hour. Serve warm.

## Mrs. AnnieBelle Brewster Berry's Fruit Sherbet

Another family recipe from Polk County, Georgia. My grandmother AnnieBelle was "Mrs. Berry to you, and you'd best not forget it!" to everyone except VERY close family members, and certainly to anyone under 50 years of age.

Juice of 3 oranges
Juice of 3 lemons
1 small can crushed pineapple, drained
1 cup water
½ cup sugar
2 egg whites

Combine orange juice, lemon juice, and pineapple.

Boil water and sugar until it spins a thread. (This is about 230° F if you use a candy thermometer.) Cool slightly, then mix with the juices and pineapple. Freeze until mushy.

Meanwhile, beat 2 egg whites until they form peaks. Fold into the mushy fruit mixture, and return to the freezer for a couple of hours.

**Note:** Very good on warm summer evenings.

## MERV DYMALLY

Two of my good friends in the political arena, Merv Dymally and Ed Soesman, introduced me to Caribbean food. I worked with Merv as his deputy chief of staff during the sixties and seventies. Ed was a political consultant and a campaign coordinator. As I look back, we only lost one election, that being Merv's second run at the California lieutenant governorship: During his first-term campaign as Jerry Brown's running mate, we kept pictures of Merv out of the press and campaign materials as much as possible, figuring what white voters didn't know about Merv's ethnicity wouldn't hurt us. Four years later, however, with Merv often acting as governor in Jerry Brown's absence, we couldn't obscure the fact that Merv was black. Racism won—we lost.

Sometimes there is a ridiculously humorous side to racism. One evening while Merv was acting governor, we attended a political rally in Orange County where Merv was slated to speak. As we walked in, the master of ceremonies rushed up to me and gushed, "Oh Governor, we're so thrilled and privileged to have you as our featured speaker!" I pointed to Merv and said, "This is the governor." The dude's jaw dropped a foot!

Merv is a product of Trinidad and Tobago. Included here are one West Indian recipe and one Creole dish contributed by Merv's wife, Alice. I was exposed to a lot of Caribbean food during Merv's campaign functions when his Trinidadian friends and relatives cooked up many tasty West Indian goodies.

## New Orleans Creole Jambalaya

Serves 4

2 pounds whole shrimp
2 tablespoons butter
1 cup onion, chopped
½ cup green pepper, chopped
2 cloves garlic, minced
¼ pound ham, chopped
1 16-ounce can tomatoes, drained (reserve liquid)
1 cup rice
3 bay leaves
¼ teaspoon dried thyme
2 tablespoons parsley, chopped
1 tablespoon celery, chopped
1 teaspoon salt
¼ teaspoon cayenne pepper
1 tablespoon Worcestershire sauce

Peel, de-vein, and wash shrimp.

Melt butter in 3-quart saucepan over medium heat. Add onion and green pepper, and sauté until soft. Stir in garlic and ham and sauté 5 minutes. Chop drained tomatoes, stir in, and cook 2 minutes. Stir in rice to blend. Add shrimp and remaining ingredients. Measure reserved tomato liquid and add hot water to equal 1½ cups. Pour liquid over all and bring to boil. Do not stir. Cover and cook over low heat for 45 minutes.

## Trinidad Curried Chicken

2 tablespoons vegetable oil
1 whole chicken, cut up
2 teaspoons salt, plus a little extra
1 teaspoon black pepper, plus a little extra
3 tablespoons curry powder, plus a little extra
1 large onion, chopped
2 cups water
2 cloves garlic, chopped
2 tablespoons celery, chopped
1 bay leaf

Heat the vegetable oil in large skillet. Season chicken with a little salt and pepper and pat with a little curry powder. Brown chicken in oil evenly on all sides without burning. Transfer chicken to a plate.

Add onions to oil, and cook for about 5 minutes or until onions are soft and transparent. Dissolve curry powder in 1 cup water and add to skillet along with garlic, celery, salt, and pepper, stirring constantly.

Return chicken and any juices that have accumulated to the skillet, stir in 1 cup water and bay leaf, and bring to boil. Reduce heat to low, cover tightly, and simmer for about 1 hour. Remove bay leaf before serving.

## LAURA JOHNSON

My daughters, Janice and Laura, married a pair of identical twins, Tony and Michael Johnson. They went from being Otises to being Johnsons. Ever since they were little girls, I've had fun cooking for them. During the 1960s, when the British bands invaded America with their synthetic form of rhythm and blues, they swept us off the scene, and I—and many of the original black R&B inventors—had a hell of a time earning a living. Phyllis landed a job at the Los Angeles branch of the United Nations, and I became the daytime custodian of our kids: Janice, Laura, Shuggie, and baby Nicky. As a result, I did a lot of cooking for the gang. For our midday meals, I'd concoct something as tasty as possible with leftovers. Actually, leftovers are just fine, but sometimes, as in this case, it was an economic necessity. I started calling the dishes Super-Dooper Daddy-O's. We'd have Daddy-O Beans and Rice, Daddy-O Hash, Daddy-O Pasta, and Daddy-O whatever last night's leftovers dictated.

The Super-Dooper Daddy-O experience may have something to do with the fact that all of our children like to cook. I've included recipes here from all four of them, plus dishes by grandson Lucky.

## "La La" Fried Chicken

My daughter Laura (we call her La La) was hesitant about submitting her fried chicken recipe. She writes: "Dear Dad, I wasn't going to compete with Mom's fried chicken, which, in my opinion, is the world's greatest, but your grandchildren, Chris, Nicole, and Kevin, and your GREAT grandchildren, Kayla and Jhlequa, insisted. I guess all kids think their mother's fried chicken is the greatest."

2 to 3 pounds chicken thighs or drumettes
Seasoned salt
Black pepper
Onion powder
Vegetable oil
1½ cup all-purpose flour

Wash chicken parts and dry on paper towels. Lightly season with Lawry's seasoned salt, black pepper, and onion powder.

Heat oil in large cast-iron skillet. Add more Lawry's, black pepper, and onion powder to flour. Put seasoned flour in brown paper bag (lunch size). Drop each piece of chicken into the bag and shake until coated, and then fry them in hot oil. Do not crowd chicken pieces. Brown about 20 minutes each side (drumettes about 10 minutes each side). As each piece is done, remove it from skillet and place on plate covered with paper towels to drain excess oil.

**Low-Fat Version (Convection Roasting Oven):**
Follow seasoning of chicken and flour as above. Put 1 cup oil in shallow plate. After shaking chicken in brown bag, lay chicken in oil, turning to cover both sides. Lay chicken on paper towels to drain excess oil. Place chicken pieces on top rack of convection roasting oven. Cook 15 minutes on each side.

## PRESTON LOVE

To his inner circle of friends and family, Preston Love is as well-known for his cooking as he is for being a world-class alto sax musician. His specialty is Omaha Barbecue. In the late 1960s, Preston had a popular LP recording titled *Omaha Barbecue*. Every cut on the album had a title related to food: "Neck Bones," "Chili Mac," "Hoe Cakes & Sorghum," "Chicken Gumbo," etc. Also included was "Shuggie's Chittlin' Blues," which helped establish my son Shuggie, 14 years old at the time, as a blues/rock guitar virtuoso.

## Down-Home Corn Bread

2 cups white cornmeal
1 cup all-purpose flour
⅔ teaspoon salt
1 heaping teaspoon baking powder
1½ cups milk, or enough to make soupy wet
1 cup bacon grease or any melted shortening
1 large or 2 small eggs

Preheat oven to 350°. Mix all dry ingredients in mixing bowl. Add milk and eggs, stirring until all is well mixed. Heat grease or shortening in baking pan until it is quite hot.

Pour grease into soupy mixture while stirring rather vigorously until it is all mixed thoroughly. Pour batter into still-warm baking pan. Bake on bottom rack of oven until corn bread has risen and is dry on top. Place on top rack of oven and bake until golden brown.

**Note:** Hot grease will sizzle when you pour it into the batter. Don't concern yourself about that.

## Jive Sweet Potato Pie

Enough for 6-inch pie. No top crust; only bottom.

3 medium-size yams
2 eggs, lightly beaten
1½ cups sugar
½ stick butter, melted
¼ teaspoon mace
½ teaspoon lemon extract
1 teaspoon vanilla
1½ cups milk

Boil yams until tender; peel and mash. Add remaining ingredients to yams and mix thoroughly.

Pour in crust and bake at 350° for 1½ hours. Be sure pie is well cooked—"candied."

### Pie Crust:

1½ cups flour for each 9-inch crust
½ teaspoon baking powder
½ teaspoon salt
¾cup cold water
¾ cup shortening or lard (lard tastes better)

Sift all dry ingredients in bowl. Cut in shortening with pastry cutter and gradually add water, cutting it into dry mixture. Dough must not be very wet, just wet enough to hold crust together.

## Preston's Omaha Barbecue

Marinate slab of pork spareribs by sprinkling with: garlic powder, salt, pepper, celery salt, and paprika. This can be done from 15 minutes to ½ hour prior to placing ribs on smoker or in barbecue pit. Cook ribs, turning constantly, until quite tender.

**Note:** Ribs can be prepared earlier by cutting off excess fat and tough parts from top of slab.

**Barbecue Sauce:**
4 cups of water, with 3 tablespoons of bottled smoke sauce added
1 cup tomato ketchup
1 cup tomato paste
1 teaspoon garlic powder (not garlic salt)
¼ teaspoon pepper flakes (not powdered)
½ teaspoon celery salt or celery seed
½ teaspoon black pepper
1 teaspoon salt
2 tablespoons brown sugar
1 large bay leaf
2 tablespoons bacon drippings
½ stick of butter (optional)

Combine ingredients and boil mixture on low flame for 1 ½ hours. Be sure to baste ribs with sauce while cooking to get full flavor.

## Pork Steak

2 thick-cut pork steaks
Salt and pepper
2 cups flour (approximately)
1 teaspoon paprika
1½ cups hot oil or shortening
1 medium-size onion, sliced
5 cups water
1 tablespoon soy sauce
1 tablespoon Worcestershire sauce
A few (6 to 8) pepper flakes (optional)

Cut pork steaks into four equal pieces. Salt and pepper each piece liberally. Shake meat in paper sack containing 1 cup of the flour mixed with paprika. Place meat in skillet with hot grease, turning occasionally until steak pieces are dark brown and crisp. Remove meat from skillet.

Make a roux (gravy) by adding ½ cup flour, stirring to keep from burning. Add the onion, stirring constantly. (Be careful not to overcook the onions or brown the mixture too much.) Add the water, soy sauce, Worcestershire sauce, and pepper flakes, still stirring constantly to avoid lumping and to keep the gravy smooth.

Return the pork steaks to the skillet. Cook over medium heat, adding cold water when needed to keep the gravy loose and until pork is very tender.

Serve over creamy mashed potatoes or rice.

## Soulful Peach Pie

Filling for Soulful Peach Pie or Peach Cobbler:

1 ½ cups sugar
½ teaspoon almond extract
½ stick butter
Dash of cinnamon and nutmeg
1 heaping teaspoon flour
1 large can freestone peaches in heavy syrup
    (not cling peaches)
Pie crust, top and bottom
    (Preston's recipe, see page 40)

Combine sugar and flour. Add all other ingredients, including can of peaches. Pour into 9-inch pie crust. Add top crust, puncturing it five times with a fork.

Place in 350° oven on bottom rack. Cook for 1 hour. Move pie to top rack, and cook for another ½ hour or until quite brown.

## Unbelievable Banana Bread

1 cup sugar
1 stick butter (margarine can be used,
    but butter is preferred)
2 eggs
2 medium-size very ripe bananas (ripened until quite
    dark and moist), mashed
1 ¼ cups all-purpose flour
¼ teaspoon salt
1 level teaspoon baking soda (NOT baking powder)
1 cup English walnuts

Cream sugar and butter in electric mixer. Add eggs
and mix thoroughly. Add flour, salt, baking soda, and
walnuts to wet mixture, and mix. Add bananas.

Butter a bread pan to prevent sticking. (It is
important to use a deep pan, the type used for
loaves.) Pour in mixture and cook in the center of a
preheated 350° oven for 45 minutes.

**Note:** Be careful not to use more than the prescribed
amount of baking soda (1 level teaspoon only). Too
much baking soda will impart an objectionable taste.
A cup of raisins may be added to the mix if desired.

## GAIL "LITTLE BIT" MULDROW

The most authentic Red Beans and Rice I've had in recent years was prepared by my feature female vocalist, Gail. She cooks the dish the way I remember it 30–40 years ago in the Deep South. She learned how to do it from her mom, a native of Louisiana. Here is the recipe with no added fanciness . . . just down-to-earth, poor-folks style.

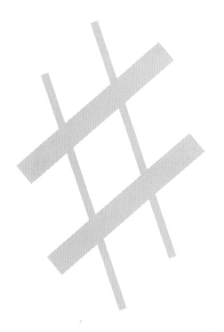

### Gail Muldrow's Red Beans and Rice

4 large ham hocks
1 ½ pounds red kidney beans
3 bay leaves
4 cloves garlic, chopped
Salt and black pepper to taste
⅓ teaspoon cayenne pepper

Preboil the ham hocks for 40 minutes. Put all ingredients in a heavy pot, and cover with water. Cook over high heat until the beans are done, stirring constantly to avoid beans sticking. Add water as necessary.

Cool pot and store in refrigerator overnight. Reheat the following day, and serve over white rice.

## TOM REED

"The Master Blaster"

Tom Reed, known in disc jockey circles as "The Master Blaster," has gone from radio broadcasting to television production and writing. His award-winning *For Members Only* TV show has received critical acclaim. In 1997, the program will have run consecutively for seventeen years, making it the longest-running African American program in California history.

In December 1992, Reed published the definitive volume on Los Angeles African American music. The mainstream publishing houses thought it was too big (coffee table size), and they complained that it contained too many pictures. Tom published the book himself. He is now into his third printing. (So much for the experts.) The book is titled *The Black Music History of Los Angeles . . . Its Roots* and can be obtained by calling (919)894-8880.

### The Master Blaster's Lean Greens

4 bunches collard greens, chopped
½ cup cider vinegar
3 cloves garlic, minced
2 red onions, chopped
½ cup salt pork
**Garnish:** tomatoes

Wash collard greens. Soak well.

Boil water slowly for 20 minutes. Then add collard greens, garlic, onions, and vinegar.

Cut salt pork into small pieces and add to the mix. Let everything cook/boil slowly for about 5 hours.

Remove the salt pork, but not until you are ready to eat your serving.

Once the greens are on the plate, slice some tomatoes on top of them. (Oh, yes, take the seeds out of the tomatoes.) Add some Tabasco sauce, if needed.

## ED SOESMAN

Ed Soesman was born in what was formerly Dutch Guiana (today known as Surinam). His wife Bettye has become skilled at Surinamese cuisine.

### Bettye Soesman's Cabbage and Okra

1 head cabbage, shredded
Several strips bacon
1 green bell pepper, sliced
1 red bell pepper, sliced
1 medium onion, sliced
2 or 3 cloves garlic, minced
1 16-ounce package frozen okra, sliced
Salt and pepper to taste

Place shredded cabbage in large pot with about ½ cup water. Fry bacon in skillet 'til crisp. Remove bacon and break into bits. Sauté bell peppers, onion, garlic, and okra in bacon fat. Add sautéed vegetables to cabbage. Stir and cook for 8 to 10 minutes. Season with salt and pepper as desired. Add bacon bits.

**Note:** Ham may be substituted for bacon and also gives good flavor.

## Surinamese Red Beans and Rice

1 pound red beans
Salt pork (rinse the salt off)
Seasoning ham
1 tablespoon margarine
1 onion
1 tomato
1 stalk celery
1 tablespoon tomato puree
1 fresh chile pepper
3 bouillon cubes
1 teaspoon nutmeg
1 tablespoon sugar
1 teaspoon black pepper

Cook beans until almost done. Cut salt pork and ham in pieces. In the margarine, sauté meat, onion, and tomato. Add to beans. Add celery, tomato puree, fresh chile, bouillon cubes, nutmeg, sugar, and black pepper. Simmer 'til tender.

 Serve over cooked rice, with Slaw (raw salad).

Slaw:
1 cucumber
1 head cabbage
Green onions
1 tomato
2 eggs, hard-boiled
⅓ cup vinegar
1 cup mayonnaise
1 tablespoon salt

Finely chop cucumbers, cabbage, and green onions. Cut tomato and eggs in small pieces. Toss with a mixture of vinegar, mayonnaise, and salt in a large salad bowl.

## JAN VAN TERSCH

Jan Van Tersch is a music fan who salutes the rock-and-roll duo Don and Dewey with this recipe.

---

### Esquerita's Chocolate-Bourbon Cake

1 package chocolate fudge or devil's food cake mix
3 eggs
⅓ cup bourbon (your choice)
½ cup oil
1 cup water
2 bars unsweetened chocolate, chopped
4 ounces semisweet chocolate chips

Mix cake mix, eggs, water, bourbon, and oil for 2 minutes. Add chopped chocolate and chips to batter.

Pour into two round 8-inch or 9-inch cake pans, and bake per directions on cake mix box. Cool 10 minutes, and then take out of pans and let cool completely on wire racks.

Put together and cover with Don and Dewey's Mocha-Bourbon Frosting.

### Mocha-Bourbon Frosting:

1 16-ounce package confectioners' sugar
6 tablespoons butter, softened
½ cup cocoa
⅓ cup hot bourbon (your choice) and hot coffee combination
½ teaspoon vanilla
⅛ teaspoon salt

In large bowl, with spoon or mixer, beat all ingredients until smooth, adding more hot coffee if necessary to make frosting spreadable.

## Jan Van Tersch's Red Beans and Rice

Serves 12

2 cups chicken broth
8 ounces dried kidney beans (about 1 cup)
3 slices bacon, cut up
1 medium onion, chopped
1 green bell pepper, chopped
White wine
1 cup white rice, uncooked
1 ½ teaspoons salt

Heat broth and beans to boil in 3-quart saucepan; boil 2 minutes. Remove from heat, cover, and let stand 1 hour. Add more broth/water to cover beans, if necessary. Heat to boiling; reduce heat, cover, and simmer until tender, 1 to 1 ½ hours. (Do not boil, or beans will burst.) Drain; reserve liquid.

Fry bacon in small skillet until crispy. Add onion and bell pepper. Cook, stirring until onion is tender. Add more chicken broth and white wine to reserved liquid to equal 2 cups. Add reserved liquid, bacon, onion, green pepper, rice, and salt to beans in 3-quart saucepan. Heat to boiling, stirring once or twice; reduce heat. Cover and simmer 14 minutes. (Do not lift cover or stir.) Remove from heat. Fluff lightly with fork; cover and let steam 5 to 10 minutes.

## DOROTHY CHESSARI

Dorothy is my sister. If you're into Middle Eastern delicacies, you'll enjoy these delicious tidbits.

### Baklava

2 cups chopped nuts
½ cup sugar
1 teaspoon cinnamon
1 pound butter, melted
1 package filo pastry sheets

Combine nuts, sugar, and cinnamon. Using a pastry brush, brush a 13-by-9-by-2-inch baking pan well with melted butter. Separate filo sheets. Place under smooth, damp towel to prevent drying. Place one filo sheet in pan. Brush with butter. Repeat for five layers of filo, brushing each layer with butter. Sprinkle ¼ of nut mixture over buttered sheets.

Repeat procedure until filo and nuts are all used up. End with filo on top. Drizzle butter over top, and sprinkle with cinnamon. Cut through this BEFORE baking in a diagonal manner to create a diamond pattern. Bake in 300° oven for 1 to 1½ hours or until golden brown. When baked, immediately pour syrup (recipe follows) over baklava.

**Syrup:**
2½ cups sugar
1¾ cups water
1 cup honey

Combine sugar and water, and bring to a boil. Simmer uncovered about 5 minutes to thicken syrup slightly. Remove from heat. Stir in honey, and cool to room temperature. Pour over hot baklava. Serve the next day.

**Note:** Do not remove from pan until next day. The syrup will be absorbed, and the baklava will not be dry.

## Kooloorokia

Small, bagel-shaped pastry

1 pound sweet butter (unsalted)
12 eggs, beat yolks and whites separately
16 cups flour (approx.)
8 teaspoons baking powder
1 teaspoon baking soda
4 cups sugar
¼ cup whiskey
2 teaspoons cinnamon
Juice from 1 orange
Sesame seeds (optional)
Cream

Combine butter and sugar. Add egg yolks and whites. Add dry ingredients, whiskey, orange juice, and cinnamon. (When adding flour, do not make dough too stiff. When you think it feels right, roll out a piece and see how it works. This dough all has to be done by hand, not in a mixer. It's a hands-on recipe in the true sense of the word.)

Let the dough sit about ½ hour, covered. Then roll out cookie dough by hand, and cut into long ½-inch strips. Shape strips into doughnut. Brush tops with cream, sprinkle with sesame seeds (optional), and bake on greased cookie sheets in 350° oven about 20 minutes or until light brown.

## Koorabiethes

Makes 3 small, boat-shaped pastries

1 pound sweet butter (unsalted)
⅔ cups powdered sugar
Pinch baking soda
1 egg yolk, well beaten
⅛ cup whiskey
4¼ cups flour (approx.)
Whole cloves (or ¼ teaspoon ground cloves)

Beat butter until thick and creamy and very light in color. Add sugar, baking soda, egg yolks, whiskey, and flour. (Add flour slowly. Do not make dough too stiff, but be sure you have added enough flour or cookies will spread and be too flat. They have to be firm when you turn them over.)

Shape by rolling in hands into a log about 2 inches thick and 6 inches long. For oval cookies, cut dough into 3 pieces on diagonal; for round cookies, cut straight across. (Cookies should be 2 inches thick.) Put a clove in the middle of each cookie, or if you're afraid someone will choke, just add the ground cloves to the batter. (This is what I do—it's safer and tastes just as good.)

Bake on greased cookie sheet in slow oven (300°) about 30 minutes until lightly browned on bottom (lift cookies to check). When finished, transfer immediately to paper towels that have been sprinkled with powdered sugar. Sprinkle tops thoroughly with more powdered sugar—they should be thick with sugar. Cool completely before serving.

## DIMITRI "JIM" KATSANOS

My good friend Jim is a building contractor/ flamenco guitarist and talented chef.

### Avgolemono Soup

1 4 to 5 pound stewing chicken
1 cup white rice
4 eggs, separated
Juice of 2 lemons

Place chicken in heavy kettle. Cover with water, simmer with lid on over a low heat until tender. Remove chicken, strain broth, and skim off fat.

Return 2 cups of the broth to heat and bring to a boil; add rice and simmer until rice is done, about 20 minutes.

Beat egg whites until stiff. Add egg yolks, one at a time, and continue beating. Gradually beat in lemon juice. Slowly add 2 cups of hot broth to egg-lemon mixture, stirring constantly. Slowly stir egg-lemon mixture into rest of soup mixture.

Serve chicken meat separately.

## Dolmathes

Stuffed grape leaves

4 large onions, chopped fine
1 cup olive oil
2 cups rice
1½ pounds ground beef or ground lamb
Juice of 2 lemons
½ cup mint leaves
Salt and pepper
2 cups beef broth (or bouillon cubes)
1 quart grape leaves

Brown ground meat and drain fat. Sauté onions in ½ cup olive oil. Add rice and stir until golden. Add onion-rice mixture to ground meat. Add juice of 1 lemon, mint, salt, pepper, and 1 cup of beef broth. Mix thoroughly.

Rinse and drain grape leaves, remove stems, and separate leaves. To fill leaves, place shiny side down, add one teaspoon of mixture, fold top of leaf over mixture, and then fold both sides inward and roll. Place seam side down in bottom of large saucepan that has been lined with grape leaves.

Place dolmathes close together, and continue to layer until all dolmathes are placed in pan. Squeeze remaining lemon juice over dolmathes, and add 1 cup of beef broth to barely cover dolmathes. Add more water if necessary. Cover with a heavy plate and simmer for 45 minutes or until rice is cooked. Serve hot or cold.

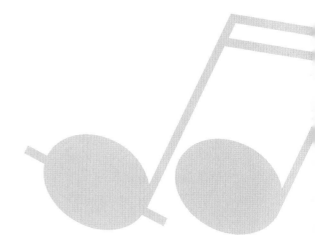

## OREKTIKA

(Appetizers)

What many Greeks have in common is their love of food ... and the celebration (*glendi*) that goes with eating.

One of the most important of the Greek food festivities is what is known as *Orektika.* "Appetizers" is a close translation of the *Orektika,* but what the word really means is "desirable" (from *orexis*), for the Greek has a desire to eat and drink while engaging in heart-warming conversation with those around him. The primary purpose of eating is not filling the stomach but partaking in a celebration of the eating process. Eating with others and sharing in the delight of warm crusty bread with miniature servings of the Greeks' favorite foods and good wines is an experience shared with the gods of Olympus.

Every region of Greece, from the high Pindus Mountains to the Ionian and Aegean Islands, has its own favorite *orektika.* I've selected four recipes here out of hundreds as the most favorite of all Greeks.

| Melitzana Salata |

Eggplant salad

2 large eggplants
½ cup olive oil
Juice of 2 lemons
Salt and pepper to taste
4 cloves garlic, crushed
1 onion, chopped fine

Bake eggplant in 350° oven for 1 hour. Remove skin and seeds. Place eggplant in blender, and mix with remaining ingredients until smooth and creamy. Serve chilled.

## Skorthalia

Dip

This garlic sauce is used plain with crusty bread or placed on cooked greens: wild dandelions, turnip, or beet; tops fish too.

8 to 10 cloves garlic
4 large white potatoes, boiled, peeled, and mashed
1 cup olive oil
1 cup vinegar or the juice of 2 lemons
Salt to taste

Crush garlic and add potatoes. Place in blender, and slowly add oil and vinegar while blending until consistency is thick and creamy.

## Taramosalata

Carp fish roe (available at Greek deli)
1 10-ounce jar of tarama
½ cup olive oil
1½ cups salad oil
10 slices white bread, crust removed
Juice of 3 lemons
1 tablespoon onions, minced
1 tablespoon parsley, minced

Boil fish roe 10 minutes and drain off water. Put tarama in cheesecloth, and rinse in cold water. Put the oils in a salad bowl. Break the bread into small pieces and place in the oil. Place all the above in an electric blender and blend. Add 1 tablespoon of the lemon juice as you mix, then fold in the onion and parsley. If mixture is too thick, add cold water. Serve with crusty bread and squirts of lemon juice.

## Tiropita

Cheese rolls in filo dough

6 eggs, separated
1 pound feta cheese, crumbled
1 pound ricotta cheese (or cottage cheese)
2 pounds filo dough
1 pound butter, melted

Beat egg yolks, add feta cheese, and mix well. Add ricotta cheese. Mix well; fold in stiffly beaten egg whites.

Take filo dough out of box, and unroll onto a moist towel. Use ¼-inch thickness of filo, cut into 3-inch squares. Place 1 teaspoon of filling in center of each square. Dampen edges with water, and fold into triangles. Cut two small slits in the top of each triangle. Brush with butter, place on a cookie sheet, and bake in a preheated 350° oven for 15 minutes or until golden brown.

## Spanakopita

Spinach dish

Makes 40 squares

3 pounds spinach
½ pound filo pastry (about 16 sheets)
½ pound butter, melted
1 cup grated Romano cheese
1½ pounds feta cheese, crumbled
½ cup olive oil
1 cup mint, chopped
1 cup milk
6 eggs, beaten

Wash spinach well; drain, and squeeze out excess water. Layer ½ of pastry sheets, each brushed with melted butter, on the bottom of 15-by-10-inch baking pan.

Combine cheeses, oil, mint, milk, beaten eggs, and spinach. Mix thoroughly, and pour on top of pastry sheets. Top with remaining pastry sheets, buttering each and top sheet as well. Bake 10 minutes in 400° oven; reduce heat to 350° and bake 1 hour longer or until brown.

## LETTIE ARIAS

Lettie Arias is a family friend who is a wonderful cook. I especially like her Cosido Soup. I remember having *cosido* in Spain a few years back. I mentioned this to Lettie, who is Mexican American, and she reminded me that much of Mexican culture is derived from Spain. Of course, the influence of Native American culture, mixed with Spanish, is what has created the wonderful Mexican dishes I love so well. In addition to *cosido,* Lettie does great *menudo,* and her tacos, tamales, and enchiladas are tops also.

### Cosido Soup

5 short ribs
3 soup bones
2 beef shanks
2 ears fresh corn, cut in halves
2 tablespoons salt
2 celery spears cut into 3 inch pieces
½ small head cabbage
2 cloves garlic, sliced
3 tomatoes, peeled
½ large onion, cut in quarters
¼ teaspoon fresh cilantro
1 tablespoon vegetable oil
3 white potatoes, cut into 1½-inch cubes
4 carrots, cut into 2-inch pieces
3 zucchini, cut into 3-inch pieces

Boil 1½ gallons of water in a heavy-gauge pot. Add meat, corn, and salt, and boil for 1 hour. Add celery, cabbage, and garlic. Fry tomatoes, onion, and cilantro in 1 tablespoon vegetable oil for 5 minutes and then add to pot. Bring pot back to a boil. Add potatoes, carrots, and zucchini, and cook for 30 minutes. Add more hot water while cooking if needed. Serve piping hot with buttered white flour tortillas and salsa.

## ROSIE "ANGEL BABY" HAMLIN
(Rosie of the Originals)

As a pretty teenager in the 1950s with a big hit record, Rosie appeared often on my Los Angeles–based television show. When I got to know her well enough, I mentioned the tenor sax solo on "Angel Baby." She laughed and said, "Everybody asks me about that! It's the world's worst solo. My regular sax man couldn't make the session. His mama wouldn't let him come out that day—you see, we were just kids. My guitar man offered to play the sax solo. He had only been playing for a month, and it sounds like it too!" Terrible sax solo or not, the record had great charm. Rosie sang it beautifully, and it became a million-selling gold record.

Rosie performs frequently at my annual Red Beans and Rice Family Music Festivals both in Santa Rosa and in southern California. She had this to say about her recipe contributions: "Johnny, my recipes are handed down from my grandmother and great-grandmother. They were from Chihuahua. My grandpa was from Mazatlan. These are traditional Mexican favorites. Try 'em. . . . I know you'll like them."

### Chicken Mole

Boil one chicken until half done, and then add 3 to 6 ounces chili powder (more or less according to taste). Simmer for 15 minutes, and then add 2 pinches of powdered shrimp and salt to taste.

Make a medium-thick paste with 1 cup cornstarch and water, and slowly stir into the simmering soup. Add a small pinch of garlic powder.

Continue to simmer over low heat until the chicken mole is the consistency of thin pea soup (about ½ hour). Serve with Spanish Rice and beans.

## Rosie's Chorizo

Dice 3 large potatoes, and brown in oil in a covered pan 'til soft. Add ½ link of pork or beef chorizo (your choice). Stir and cook with potatoes until chorizo is broken into little crumbled bits and well cooked (about 20 minutes).

Scramble 4 or 5 eggs into chorizo until done.

Serve with warm flour tortillas or wrapped in a tortilla burrito style.

## Spanish Rice

Heat 2 tablespoons of oil in a cast-iron skillet. Add 2 cups of rice, and stir constantly until rice is evenly browned. Add 1 cup chopped onion, and sauté. Add 1 cup tomato sauce and salt to taste, and stir. Add 1 cup of chicken stock and 3 cups water. Add 1 pinch of powdered shrimp, and simmer over low heat until done, about 25 minutes.

Serve with whole or refried pinto beans and warm tortillas.

# PHYLLIS OTIS

In 1945, I landed the coveted job of house band at the Club Alabam on Central Avenue in Los Angeles. It was a great opportunity. The band totaled 16 members, including vocalists Ernestine Anderson and Bing Williams. The Trenier Twins were part of that ensemble also, as were musicians Paul Quinechette, Teddy Buckner, Bill Doggett, Curtis Counce, Howard Martin, Kent Pope, Von Streeter, Loyal Walker, and Sonny "Mushmouth" Graven. Charlie Parker, Slim Gaillard, Ben Webster, Lester Young, and Miles Davis would often drop by and sit in. There were other musicians, of course, but I just thought I'd do a little name-dropping.

We spent two exciting years at the Club Alabam. Most of the band members and Phyllis and I lived in an old apartment building I rented on Washington Boulevard near Hoover. The gig paid $55 a week for side man and $75 for bandleader. That sounds like starvation wages today, but it was Musicians Union Scale, and it was, after all, fifty years ago. By budgeting carefully, we made out fine. The few druggies and alcoholics in the band were always broke, but that's the way it is when addiction claims people. We always tried to get people with unfortunate drug or alcohol habits to eat before going to work. When we were successful, the addicted musician stood a better chance of functioning artistically. It was heartbreaking to see wonderfully talented musicians unable to eat because of alcohol or hard drugs. We all smoked cigarettes in those days . . . we thought it was so cool to stand around at intermission puffing away. Most of us know better today, but that's another subject.

In addition to the rooms I provided for the members, Phyllis would cook up a hearty meal for us every day. The meals were usually spaghetti and meat balls, red beans and rice, or tamale pie. Dishes we could fill up on but didn't cost a lot to prepare. Every meal included lettuce salad, bread and butter, and red Kool-Aid. The bread was often white Wonder bread, but occasionally we had corn bread. I enjoy the healthier whole-grain breads that have become popular today, but I won't apologize for buttered supermarket white bread sopped in gravy . . . I love it!

The Club Alabam was dark on Tuesdays, and this was my day to go fishing on one of the old barges off the breakwater in San Pedro. For fifty cents, you could fish all day with plenty of free live anchovies from the big bait wells. We never failed to fill our buckets with butter-mouth perch, opal eye and pile perch, herring, tom cod (kingfish), halibut, barracuda, and a slew of other varieties. One year, salmon came into the harbor, and for three days we had a bonanza.

Wednesdays and Thursdays were our fish fry days. Even some of the spaced-out brothers showed up for those meals. I got so I could fry and bake the fish pretty good. Some of those recipes are contained in this book.

All of Phyllis's dishes were delicious, but a particular favorite with the fellows and ladies in the band was her Tamale Pie. I saw trumpeter Tony Moret in New Orleans a while back, and he asked wistfully, "Man, does Phyllis still cook up that wonderful tamale pie?"

## Tamale Pie

5 cups water
1 teaspoon salt
2½ cups cornmeal
½ cup onion, chopped
½ cup green bell pepper, chopped
2 cloves garlic, chopped
3 tablespoons vegetable oil
1½ pounds ground beef (or turkey, if preferred)
½ teaspoon chili powder
½ teaspoon cayenne pepper
1½ cans chopped tomatoes
1 16-ounce can whole kernel corn
1 can black olives
1 cup cheddar cheese, grated
2 cups corn chips, crushed

Bring salted water to a boil. Add cornmeal and cook for 5 minutes, stirring often. Sauté onion, bell pepper, and garlic in vegetable oil over medium heat about 1 minute. Add ground beef and cook until brown. Add chili powder, cayenne pepper, tomatoes, corn, and olives.

Line an oiled casserole with ¾ of the cornmeal mix. Pour in meat mixture. Sprinkle top with cheese and crushed corn chips. Dot edges with remaining cornmeal. Bake in 375° oven for approximately 30 minutes. Remove from oven when top is lightly browned.

## AMYTHEST OTIS

The traditional Native American recipes contributed by my daughter-in-law, Amythest, were handed down to her by her Lakota Sioux father. When I asked what she could contribute to the book, my son Nick urged her to go with Vegetarian Pemmican and Campfire Trout because he enjoys them so much. Unlike so many young people, Indian or otherwise, who tend to play down their cultural heritage, Amythest speaks proudly of her youth on the reservation and the traditions of her people. She offers the following description of *Wagmiza Wasna:* "This is a meatless version of the traditional pemmican. It uses parched corn in place of beef. Pemmican was used as a trade item and is still widely used on a daily basis. It is eaten during ceremonial events and given as gifts."

### Campfire Trout

Traditionally, this recipe is prepared by skewering the fish on a forked stick and cooking over a campfire. After the Europeans introduced bacon and salt, the native people began to add these ingredients to their food, along with the ancient New World seasonings of spicebush and onions.

1 whole trout
Whole ground spicebush berries (or allspice) to taste
Salt to taste
6 green onions
6 thin strips bacon

Split belly open and clean trout under cold water. Rub fish with seasonings inside and out. Stuff with onions. Tie bacon around fish so that stuffing is contained. Push a strong forked stick with a sharpened end into the belly of fish. Cook over campfire until the flesh is flaky and the bacon is done.

## Stuffed Pumpkin

The Lakota people once lived near the Great Lakes and northern woodlands, so they were familiar with the wild rice that grew there. After migrating onto the plains, they established a trade route with neighboring tribes, exchanging hides and meat for the rice.

1 5-pound pumpkin
2 teaspoons salt
½ teaspoon dry mustard
2 tablespoons vegetable oil or rendered fat
1 pound venison, buffalo, or beef (optional)
1 chopped onion
1 cup wild rice, cooked
3 eggs, beaten
1 tablespoon dried sage, crushed
¼ teaspoon black pepper

Preheat oven to 350°. Cut off top of pumpkin and remove the seeds. Run a fork over the entire inside surface of pumpkin, creating grooves in the flesh. Rub 1 teaspoon salt and mustard into grooves.

Heat oil in a large skillet. Add meat and onions, and cook over medium heat until brown. Take skillet off heat, and stir in rice, eggs, remaining salt, sage, and pepper. Stuff entire mixture into pumpkin.

Put a little water in a shallow baking pan, and place pumpkin in pan. Bake 1½ hours, adding water to pan as needed to avoid scorching. Cut in wedges and serve.

## Wagmiza Wasna

Vegetarian pemmican

2 cups yellow corn meal
1 cup dry chokeberries (or raisins)
1 cup water
⅓ cup sugar
1 cup melted suet or butter

Preheat oven to 350°. In a shallow pan, toast corn-meal until lightly browned, stirring thoroughly and often. Meanwhile, have berries or raisins soaking in water. After draining berries, mix with cornmeal and sugar. Add melted suet or butter, and stir well.

Press into 3-inch disk-like balls (or press into pan and freeze for later use). Bake in 350° oven for 45 minutes to 1 hour.

## DR. GARY HERZBERG

Years ago, in Los Angeles, I was telling my old friend, the late musician/comic Mickey Katz, that my doctor often went fishing with me. Mickey remarked that it was great to have a doctor on board in case your heart should attack you. After all these years, I've found a doctor friend up here in northern California who likes to go fishing.

Gary Herzberg reminds all of us who go fishing together that it's smart to eat healthy. Doc is not a vegetarian zealot, but he stresses fruit, vegetables, fiber, and of course, exercise. We get plenty of exercise out on Tomales Bay casting, reeling in, casting, reeling in, etc., etc. Sometimes we even make a mistake and catch something!

Tomales Bay is one of the cleanest bodies of water in America, so Gary approves when we keep and eat some of the fish we catch.

### Leah's Matzo Balls

3 eggs
2 cups matzo meal
1 ¼ cups water
1 to 2 teaspoons salt
1 to 2 tablespoons chicken fat or oil
Dash of pepper

Beat eggs lightly, then mix together all ingredients and let mixture stand for ½ hour or longer in refrigerator.

Grease hands with oil, and roll pieces of the mixture into small to medium balls. Drop them into a large quantity of boiling salted water or soup. Cover and cook for about 20 minutes.

**Note:** Balls will puff up while boiling and then deflate when taken out. This is normal.

## Teiglach in Syrup

A family treat for the holidays.

**Syrup:**
3 cups honey
2 cups sugar
2 teaspoons ginger

**Dough:**
3 cups flour
1 teaspoon baking powder
3 tablespoons sugar
1 teaspoon ginger
¼ teaspoon salt
5 eggs, well beaten
3 tablespoons oil

**Last Additions:**
1 teaspoons ginger
¾ cup hot coffee

In a large pot, combine the honey, sugar, and ginger for the syrup, stirring over a medium flame until the sugar dissolves. Bring to a boil, reduce the heat, and allow to boil gently for 10 minutes while you prepare the dough.

Combine the dry ingredients. Add the beaten eggs and oil to the dry ingredients, stirring until smooth. The dough should be soft but just stiff enough to handle. Divide the dough, and roll each part into a ½-inch rope. Tie the end of the rope into a pretzel-like knot. Cut off the knot, and continue making knots for the length of the rope. You may prefer to first cut each rope into about 4-inch pieces and then twist the pieces into knots.

Drop the knots into the boiling syrup a few at a time. To keep the syrup boiling gently, simmer covered for about 20 minutes. Remove the cover, and stir the browned *teiglach* on the top into the syrup in order to raise the *teiglach* on the bottom to the top. Keep stirring until all the *teiglach* are brown and sound hollow when tapped. To test, put one in a glass of water. If done, it should float on the surface of the water. When broken open, the inside should be dry and crisp.

Just before turning off the heat, add the hot coffee and ginger, and stir well. Let cool until easy to handle. Ladle the *teiglach* and syrup into jars while still warm. Cover when the jars are cool. The *teiglach*, if bottled correctly, will last indefinitely—that is, if there are any left.

**Note:** For variations, 2 teaspoons of grated orange rind can be added to the dough and to the syrup; or nuts and raisins may be added to the syrup with the coffee; or a large raisin could be twisted into each knot.

## JIM KOHN

Jim Kohn is the leader of an instrumental combo that features klezmer (Yiddish), Turkish, Greek, and other Middle Eastern music. He says his group "Sevastopol" is the band that put the *oy* in Joy. Included here are recipes that reflect his musical tastes.

---

### Cream Cheese Kipfel and Delchele (Pastry to Die For)

Now this is really a family recipe and makes a couple kinds of holiday pastries that will make grandma *kvell* with pride and will make everyone else overeat. First, my mother's version. She wrote out this recipe, so I'm quoting the directions.

1 cup butter or margarine
1 cup (½ pound) cream cheese
2 cups sifted enriched flour
½ teaspoon salt
½ pound nuts, chopped
4 tablespoons sugar
Cinnamon
Prune or apricot *lechvar* (a thick jam)

Using your hands, combine quickly the butter, cream cheese, flour, and salt. (When I combine the first three ingredients, I find it easier to first blend the cream cheese and margarine together and then add the flour with a dough blender like you would to make a pie crust.) Place in refrigerator overnight. Roll out dough to ¼ inch thick on floured board. Cut into 2-inch squares. Mix together nuts, sugar, and cinnamon. Place a small amount on each square and roll up. Bake in moderate 375° oven for 10 to 15 minutes.

You can also make *delchele* from this same dough. Instead of the nut mixture, place about ½ teaspoon of prune or apricot *lechvar* in center of each square. Bring each point to the center, and press down.

Other variants from my grandmother (my father's mother, this time). In double recipe, add 2 tablespoons of ice water to 4 tablespoons of heavy cream and add to the cream cheese and butter mixture. (She used sweet butter.) You can roll up the triangles—I remember they would shape these into crescents too and make little slits in the side. You can also fill with a mixture of creamed farmer cheese, butter, cream, and sugar and then add an egg and a little lemon juice. Bake until golden brown, maybe even 20 minutes. (Oy, this is making me hungry!)

## Fritata Freylekhs

Breakfast kugel

This dish can have much variety, but there's one main feature: it becomes a filling omelet-type dish with lots of veggies and a small amount of egg per portion. It also recycles leftovers like crazy. In short, it's a *mechaieh* (a real pleasure)!

You'll need a large, deep frying pan (I use an ironware one), not one of those froufrou omelet pans. It will make four to six servings, depending on how hungry everyone is and whether they're *essers* or *fressers* (eaters or face-stuffers).

### A Nice Combination of Vegetables:
Light spring varieties: spinach, zucchini, bok choy, bean sprouts, green onions, red bell peppers
Medium good-for-you stuff: broccoli, cauliflower, red or green cabbage
Winter goodies: potatoes, carrots
Leftovers: any sautéed or steamed veggies; don't forget pasta, and corn cut off the cob (oy! so good!)
Cashews, sometimes

### Always:
Olive oil
1 onion (or ½, if it's too big), chopped
4 to 6 cloves garlic, chopped (or more—don't be shy, it cures everything . . . also, you never heard of klezmer musicians having vampire problems, and it keeps club owners at a proper distance)
4 to 6 mushrooms

### Seasonings:
Ground cumin
Chile pepper (fresh) or chili powder
Worcestershire sauce
Soy sauce

### The Hold-It-Together Part:
Eggs (2 large, maybe 3 medium, or 2 of those super jumbos)
Buttermilk

Put a little olive oil and get it medium hot and *shmeered* all over in the pan. Sauté the onions, and then add heavier veggies like carrots or broccoli. If you've got three arms, you can be peeling garlic while stirring. I always use fresh garlic because it tastes the best. You can save sauté time if you steam things like broccoli and potatoes for a few minutes (or microwave, but don't let these things get too soft).

You save leftovers for later because they're already cooked, right? The idea is to cook veggies to the crunch point. Just use your *kopf*. Don't forget to add the chopped garlic and mushrooms. (Everything is sliced or diced, just like the machine on TV.) Fresh chile, maybe half depending on how spicy you like your mornings. (You can even leave out the seeds, which are hotter, but that's no fun!) When the veggies are nearly done, add some cumin and chili powder (if you didn't use fresh chiles). Stir in a few dashes of Worcestershire and large *spritzes* of soy. (I use the low-salt soy, which still has all the flavor.) Watch the heat, you shouldn't burn anything. If you like a crunchy texture, add a handful of cashew pieces about halfway

into this part—not too soon, or they'll get burned.

With your third arm, you're beating the eggs with some buttermilk. Use a good, cultured buttermilk. It's almost like yogurt, but sweeter, and makes the custard part of the dish nice and fluffy. How much? It's like a batter, not soupy. One final stir, and then add the eggs and buttermilk mixture. If you're doing this right, you'll have plenty of veggies and just enough liquid to seep around all the chunks without drowning them. You can help spread it around with a fork, but don't stir or it'll be a scramble in no time! Now lower the heat (you've probably lowered it a couple of times already when the veggies start to cook) and cover for a while. As it starts to set like a nice custard, grate some cheese on top. Your favorite, mild or sharp, or maybe combine a few. Just none of that processed *dreck*, please.

Now you watch like an eagle. If it looks too liquidy, open cover a crack. Make sure it isn't starting to burn on the bottom. (Good cooks can tell these things by paying attention to the odors.) If it hasn't set after a few minutes (or if you prefer a drier dish), put the pan under the broiler and lightly brown the top. (Don't be a *klutz*. Take the cover off when you do this!)

Cut into four to six pieces and enjoy. Depending on the chile content, we like to top it off with yogurt if it's hot and salsa if it's not. Also, since each serving has maybe half an egg at most, it's so guilt-free that Jewish people may have to put sour cream on top to make up for it!

## Kremzel

Breakfast pancakes

This is a fast and super-healthy way to make pancakes from scratch. It's just a touch of *kremzel*, which is a traditional pancake made of matzo meal at Passover time. Mine are for any time.

1 cup whole wheat flour
1 cup matzo meal (if you don't have any,
　　try cornmeal)
1 cup oat bran
Pinch of salt
½ teaspoon baking soda
½ teaspoon baking powder (if you can get baking
　　powder)
½ cup cashew pieces, chopped in a nut grinder
An egg or two
Buttermilk
Olive oil

Combine the dry ingredients. (Use a big bowl so you don't spill.) Beat the egg or two with about a cup of buttermilk, and mix into the dry stuff. It's probably too thick, right? So add more buttermilk, a little at a time until you've got a nice, loose batter. But don't put it away yet because you'll wait 5 minutes and then maybe the batter got too thick again. It's the bran and the meal that does that. So add a *bissel* more—not much please—and mix just enough to make a nice batter.

Fry large spoonfuls of the batter in hot oil (again, I use olive oil—maybe I watched too much Popeye when I was a kid), and brown on each side. The pancakes will fluff up nicely because of the buttermilk.

Eat these pancakes with maple syrup, honey, sorghum syrup, or your favorite jam. Butter optional.

## Latkes

Potato pancakes

I watched my mother and grandmother make these many times, and then I picked up a few hints from a little private cookbook put together by a temple sisterhood in Los Angeles in the fifties. Finally, I've added a few flavors and techniques of my own. And remember, it doesn't have to be Hanukkah for you to make a big stack of *heyser* (hot) latkes for everyone. It does help, however, to have a *heyser* klezmer band playing in the living room so that everyone doesn't crowd into the kitchen (because it smells so good) and drive the cook *meshugge*.

6 medium potatoes (russet, Idaho, mature brown,
    the kind that *mensch,* Luther Burbank, discovered)
1 onion
A few cloves of garlic
An egg or two
Salt
Flour
Matzo meal
Olive oil

It's important to start with mature potatoes (low moisture) and to be sure to get all the potato water out of the mix. Here's how. Grate the potatoes into a large bowl. If they're nice organic potatoes, leave the peels on (not traditional, but good for you already). Use the coarse part of the grater. (OK, you can use a food processor, but don't make potato sauce out of it. The grater is more traditional unless you're such a vegetarian you're afraid a piece of knuckle might end up in it!)

Anyway, if you push this potato pile to one side, you'll see water accumulating on the bottom. Good!

But we want more. Have another bowl handy. Start to pick up handfuls of potato (make sure your hands are clean, OK?) and squeeze. If you're from back East, it's like making snowballs. Get as much water out of the potato balls as you can, and throw them into the other bowl. (Don't let the *kinder* start a potato ball fight). When you're done, let the liquid be while you grate the onion and garlic into the potato and mix.

Now you can pour off the brownish potato water and . . . vot's dis? Some sticky stuff on the bottom of the bowl? This we want: it's potato starch and will help hold the pancakes together. Beat into this your egg or two, being sure to get all the starch loose and into the mixture. Then beat this mixture into the potatoes. To make it stick together a little more, sprinkle in some flour and, if it's handy, some matzo meal. Mix it up!

Pour a generous amount of oil in a pan. I like olive oil, but it smokes up the kitchen when it gets hot so open the back door. And get it hot so that when you add those large spoonfuls of potato, they'll brown up nice and not soak up too much oil. Flatten out those cakes plenty thin and turn when golden. Serve hot.

Applesauce was always served with these in my family, which some plopped on top of the latkes, I guess because it tastes good! No syrup because these are a dinner dish . . . But do what you want and don't worry about the oil—you don't get these every night, you know.

## STAR LAWSON

Star Lawson is a young photographer in the Sonoma County area. Included here are some recipes for mouth-watering Italian goodies she learned from her mother.

| Mom's Carlucci Cookies |
| --- |

4 pounds flour
1 pound lard (or other shortening)
1 8-ounce can cocoa
2 pounds sugar
3 tablespoons baking powder
Grated rind of 1 orange
Grated rind of 1 lemon
1 teaspoon cinnamon
1 teaspoon allspice
½ teaspoon cloves
4 cups sweetened black coffee
1 teaspoon vanilla

Work lard or shortening into flour. Mix all ingredients. Form into preferred shape. Bake in 400° oven for 10 to 12 minutes.

**Frosting:**
Mix 3 boxes powdered sugar with 1 cup boiling water. Frost cookies while they are warm.

## Pasta Primavera

**Sauté the following in olive oil:**

1 small cauliflower, chopped

1 small bunch broccoli, chopped

1 carrot, sliced

2 medium zucchini, sliced

½ medium onion, sliced

4 medium cloves garlic, minced

2 tablespoons frozen green peas
   (or snow peas, if preferred)

**White Sauce:**

2 cups milk

2 tablespoons cornstarch

4 tablespoons butter

½ teaspoon salt

¼ teaspoon black pepper

Combine milk and cornstarch, and mix until smooth. Add with remaining ingredients to the vegetables, stirring constantly. Bring to a boil, lower heat, and simmer for 2 minutes.

   Serve over hot drained pasta (approximately 1 pound).

## Star's Pesto

2 cups packed, clean basil leaves
½ teaspoon salt
3 cloves garlic
¼ cup olive oil

Blend ingredients in food processor until very smooth, adding a touch more oil if needed. Serve over pasta, toast, or pizza.

**Note:** The Americanized version adds pine nuts and parmesan cheese. In Sicily, where this recipe is from, they did not often use these ingredients because it is a poor island.

## Pizza

**Dough:**

2 cups flour
1 tablespoon shortening
½ teaspoon salt
1 teaspoon yeast
⅔ cup water

Mix all ingredients well, and knead for 3 minutes. Let rise in a covered bowl in a warm place for 30 to 45 minutes. Roll out to approximately ⅛ inch thick on a floured board.

**Sauce:**

Best if mixed ahead so flavors can blend.
1 6-ounce can tomato paste
6 ounces water
½ teaspoon salt
¼ teaspoon black pepper
⅛ teaspoon cayenne pepper
¼ teaspoon garlic powder

**Topping:**

½ cup grated mozzarella cheese
Light sprinkle of dried oregano
Light drizzle of olive oil

Spread sauce in thin layer over entire crust. Sprinkle with cheese. Add your choice of toppings. The final touch is the oregano and olive oil (very important).

Bake on a greased cookie sheet or baking stone at 450° until cheese bubbles and pizza is tinged light brown on bottom (approximately 20 minutes).

## Polenta with Vegetables

Bring 3 cups water and 1 teaspoon salt to a boil.
Slowly stir into the boiling water 1 cup cold water and
    1 cup polenta. Return to a boil, lower heat, and
    cook 'til it pulls away from sides of pot (approxi-
    mately 10 minutes).

Sauté the following vegetables in olive oil:
1 peeled eggplant, cut into in 1-inch cubes
½ cup green bell pepper, chopped
½ cup onion, chopped
2 medium zucchini, sliced
3 medium cloves garlic, minced

When mixture has simmered for 3 minutes, add
1 14-ounce can of chopped tomatoes and continue
simmering. Serve vegetables over polenta.

## NEW LENA'S CHEF MICHAEL SCOTT

Lena's restaurant in Santa Rosa has been serving wonderful Italian dishes since 1890. That tradition of excellence held true until early 1996, when, sadly, the restaurant closed down. I hope that technical difficulties are being ironed out and New Lena's will rise again!

I hope so because the months we spent playing at the supper club were really enjoyable. One of the highlights of that engagement was owner/chef Michael Scott's great cooking.

## Pork Loin Pot Roasted in Milk

Serves 4 to 6

2 to 2½ pounds loin of pork
5 tablespoons olive oil
1 sprig rosemary
2 cloves garlic
Salt
2½ cups milk

Have the pork boned, rolled, and tied. Heat oil in a heavy casserole, one into which the meat will fit snugly. Add the rosemary and garlic and then the meat and salt. Brown the meat, turning from time to time. Discard the rosemary and garlic. Pour the milk over the meat. Cover the casserole and cook for about 1 to 1½ hours.

Cut the meat into medium slices, and keep warm on a platter. Skim off as much fat as possible from sauce, bring to boil, and pour over meat.

Note: This is a traditional manner in which pork loin is cooked in Venice. There is no more succulent method. You'll love it!

## SHUGGIE OTIS

*Nothing* surpasses spaghetti as my #1 favorite dish. I can eat pasta, and especially spaghetti, every day of my life. Phyllis makes great spaghetti meals, as do my daughters, Janice and Laura. Son Nicky and grandson Lucky are good with spaghetti also, but the family champion has to be my son Shuggie. The rest of us tend to try to get fancy with new spices and herbs, but Shuggie cooks up a good old, plain old spaghetti that is mouth-watering, and he whips it up fast, which is nice when you are really hungry. He does it with or without meat, and both versions are delicious.

| Good Old, Plain Old Spaghetti |
| --- |

1 small onion, chopped
1 clove garlic, chopped
1 pound lean ground beef
2 cans tomato sauce
2 cans tomato paste
1 teaspoon salt
½ teaspoon black pepper
1 pound spaghetti, cooked

Sauté onion and garlic in a large iron skillet. Add ground beef, and cook over medium heat, being careful not to burn onions or garlic. Add tomato sauce, tomato paste, salt, and pepper, and simmer for 20 minutes. Add precooked spaghetti, and simmer together for another 10 minutes.

# NEW ENGLAND RECIPES

## WILLIAM "BLIK" AVANT

Blik was a really good cook from the time we were kids. For many years, he functioned as transportation manager for my show. We all looked forward to the great meals Blik would concoct in our hotel and motel rooms. We carried two large suitcases with all the utensils and hot plates we needed to cook with. Most hotels and motels did not allow cooking in the rooms, but we had ways of escaping detection. A wet towel stuffed across the bottom of the door would keep the aromas out of the hallway.

Once, in Boston, a hotel manager caught us dead to rights. Blik had whipped up a wonderful smothered steak and onions, mashed potatoes, collard greens, and apple cobbler feast. The manager insisted on being let into the room and we couldn't refuse. He had a bit of an attitude at first, but then he took a deep breath and said, "Oh, my God! What is that smelling so heavenly?" Every evening for two weeks, before we left for the gig, he had dinner with us. Within a few days, the two maids on the floor were dining with us too!

Blik pulled out all the stops . . . split pea soup, oxtail stew, cracklin' corn bread, neck bones and beans . . . you name it. These were northern white folks who had heard of, but had never eaten, southern soul food. Blik gave them recipes for everything. That was 25 years ago, but I'll bet that somewhere in America they're still cookin' up Blik's gastronomic goodies.

---

| New England Boiled Dinner |
|---|

Prepare this dish in a large, heavy-gauge pot.

Corned beef (can be purchased at supermarkets)
6 carrots, diced
1 head cabbage, quartered
6 medium-size white potatoes, cut into
   chunky wedges

Cook corned beef for about 4 hours or according to directions on the package. After 4 hours, remove meat from pot, and reserve stock. Add onions, potatoes, and carrots to stock, and simmer approximately 15 minutes or until vegetables are cooked but not overdone and mushy. Add cabbage and turn off heat, leaving cabbage to steam with the pot covered and off the burner.

**Note:** Do not return meat to the stock as it slices better if not too hot.

## Split Pea Soup

1 pound dried split peas
½ pound ham (can consist of leftover ham
   bone and meat or sliced ham)
2 medium-size onions, diced
3 small hot red peppers (optional)
3 cloves garlic, diced
4 stalks celery, including some leaves, finely diced
4 carrots, diced
1 medium-size white potato, diced
5 or 6 parsley sprigs
1 pinch basil
1 pinch nutmeg
1 pinch tarragon
Salt and black pepper to taste

Bring to a boil 2¾ quarts of water in a large, heavy-gauge pot. Add ham, onions, and peppers. Boil for 1 hour. Add garlic, celery, carrots, potatoes, and parsley.

Add split peas and seasonings and boil for 1 hour more or until peas are completely done.

Can be served after left standing for ½ hour but is better when refrigerated overnight. In reheating, a small amount of water may be needed.

# CHILI

## DAVID BURNS

In the heart of the little town of Sebastopol sits the Slice of Life Restaurant. Every time I eat there, I am reminded how delicious vegetarian meals can be. I am also reminded how healthy vegetarian food is.

The proprietor, David Burns, is a veritable magician when it comes to vegetarian American, Italian, and Mexican cuisine.

### Tempeh Chili

1 pound tempeh
3 cloves garlic, minced
1 large green bell pepper, chopped
1 large onion, chopped
4 tablespoons chili powder
2 tablespoons vinegar
½ teaspoon cumin
1 teaspoon coriander
1 16-ounce can stewed or crushed tomatoes
1 16-ounce container salsa
2 16-ounce cans kidney beans
Salt

Grate or finely dice tempeh, and sauté with garlic, bell pepper, and onion. Add remaining ingredients and bring to a boil. Reduce heat and simmer 30 minutes, stirring often. Add water as needed and salt to taste.

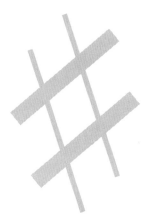

## TERRY GOULD

Over the years, I've had some pretty good band managers, but Terry is hands down the best. Just when I thought I knew everything about him, he springs his Sonoma County Chili on me. I was enjoying this great dish before we ever decided to do a cookbook. Once the book was in the works, I knew I had to include Terry's culinary masterpiece. Because his wife, Debby, is such an excellent cook, I have a sneaking suspicion that she lent a helping hand in inventing this dish—but that's what good friends and spouses are for, I suppose.

### Sonoma County Chili

5 tablespoons olive oil
2 large onions, chopped
8 cloves garlic, minced
2 pounds ground sirloin
6 cups water
3 cups canned tomatoes, cut while cooking
2 bell peppers, diced
4 15-ounce cans kidney beans, rinsed
4 15-ounce cans chili beans
2 teaspoons celery seed
1 teaspoon cayenne pepper
4 teaspoons ground cumin seed
1 large bay leaf
½ cup chili powder
1 teaspoon basil
1 tablespoon salt

Heat olive oil in skillet, add onion and garlic, and sauté until golden. Add the meat, and brown.

Transfer meat mixture into a large pot and add the remaining ingredients. Bring to a boil, reduce heat and simmer, uncovered, for about 3 hours.

Add the beans and simmer another 30 minutes.

## MARY MOORE

My friend Mary is a dedicated worker for civil and human rights in the Sonoma County area. If there is a worthy cause that deserves support, Mary will be found right in the middle of the fray fighting the good fight. From my standpoint, she's a really good cook too.

### Mary's Chili

2 pounds dried pinto beans (or whatever bean you like)
Cumin, chili pepper, and garlic salt to taste
2 medium onions
1 large bell pepper (green or red)
Several cloves of garlic
Chile peppers (canned or fresh)
Olive oil
Lean ground beef (optional)
2 large cans tomatoes or a dozen fresh tomatoes
Salsa (to taste)
1 can beef broth
Hot sauce (optional and to taste)

Rinse and soak the beans overnight in water with spices added.

Chop and dice the onions, bell pepper, garlic, and chiles. Sauté veggies in olive oil until limp and well blended. Add ground beef if you wish, and sauté 'til done. Add another round of spices. (You can use packaged chili mix here.) Add tomatoes, salsa sauce, beef broth, and water, and simmer for a couple of hours. While stirring, chant: "Down with racism, sexism, and classism! Up with justice!"

Ask Johnny for tips on hot sauce and use discreetly.

**Note:** This recipe will feed a whole bunch of people. Serve at fund-raisers, benefits, and those endless meetings where people need to stay awake!!

## RAY "BAIT BOY" BURROWS

Ray Burrows is a fishing buddy of mine. He got the name "Bait Boy" a few years ago when six of us went out to Tomales Bay after halibut and salmon. Ray was in charge of buying the bait. He bought exactly one package of frozen anchovies. They lasted for ½ hour. We were pissed! As punishment for his nefarious deed we dubbed him "Bait Boy." He's not much good at buying bait, but I will admit he does an excellent job of cooking fish, as the following recipes will attest.

### Bait Boy's Poached Lingcod

1 whole lingcod (15 to 20 inches long)
2 small lemons
Pinch of fresh dill
Pinch of fresh basil
About 1 cup water

Small lingcod are highly prized in many eastern cultures for their delicate, almost sweet flavor. The key to preserving this light flavor is to poach the cod for a very short period of time (no more than 7 to 10 minutes).

Fillet your lingcod into two pieces, making a single fillet out of each side. Place in an small poaching pan (about 2 quarts) and fill with water to a level just below the poaching rack (about ½ inch short). Squeeze the juice of 1 lemon over the fish, and then sprinkle your tiny bit of dill and basil over the fillets. Slice the remaining lemon into small rounds, and garnish the fillets. Cover your pan and poach on high for 7 to 10 minutes (or until meat easily flakes with the touch of a fork). The light, arresting aroma of dill, basil, and lemon will fill your kitchen as the fish poaches. Fish fanciers often cite this dish as one of their favorites.

**Note:** Small red potatoes steamed with tiny bits of garlic and small sprigs of cilantro make an excellent side dish.

## Halibut and/or Salmon Barbecue

Fresh garlic
Butter
Fresh lemon
1 medium-to-large halibut or salmon, whole

Sauté garlic in melted butter. Put fish on tin foil; cover
fish with the sautéed garlic and melted butter.
Squeeze lemon juice on top. Seal tin foil, and place on
barbecue. Close lid. Cook until done.

## Largemouth Bass

Serves 4

4 bass fillets
Milk
Flour
Canola oil
Garlic salt
⅓ cup fresh or concentrated lemon juice

Dip fillets in milk. Coat with flour. Fry filets in 1/4 inch
of canola oil. Sprinkle with garlic salt. Pour lemon juice
on top of fish. Cover with lid, and cook for about 30 to
60 seconds, until juice is absorbed. Fish is ready to eat!

## Sturgeon Fry

6 thinly sliced sturgeon steaks
2 eggs, beaten
Italian-style Progresso bread crumbs
Canola oil
Salt and pepper

Dip steaks in eggs and roll in bread crumbs. Fry in oil.
Do not overcook. Add salt and pepper to taste.
Almost as good as abalone!

## ORRAL AND JOAN CRAG

Orral and I have traded vegetable seeds through the years. One day, he sent me this recipe.

### Cabbage and Beef Soup

Yield: 3 quarts

1 pound lean ground beef
½ teaspoon garlic salt
¼ teaspoon garlic powder
¼ teaspoon pepper
2 celery stalks chopped
1 16-ounce kidney beans, undrained
½ medium head cabbage, chopped
1 28-ounce can tomatoes, chopped, liquid reserved
3½ cups water
4 beef bouillon cubes
Chopped parsley (fresh if available)

In a Dutch oven, brown beef. Add all remaining ingredients except parsley, and bring to a boil. Reduce heat and simmer, covered, for 1 hour. Garnish with parsley.

**Note:** Soup can be frozen in serving-size portions to enjoy months later.

## DR. GEORGE CURTIS

Dr. George is the pharmacist heard on my KPFA radio show every Saturday morning dispensing good health advice and not-so-good corny jokes. He is also an amateur chef par excellence. Dr. George says, "Medicine and cooking are very much alike; they are both arts, and no two treatments of a patient or a meal are quite the same."

## Garlic-Fennel Pork Chops with Mushrooms

Serves 4

Pork, the other white meat! I'm not sure that marketing slogan is one of my favorites, but this recipe will be one of yours! The combined flavors of sautéed garlic and fennel with lean pork chops will spice up your kitchen.

4 lean center-cut pork chops at least ¾ inch thick
Salt and pepper
2 tablespoons whole fennel seeds
2 tablespoons olive oil
5 large cloves garlic, crushed and chopped
½ cup white wine
6 large Crimini or button mushrooms, sliced

Bring pork chops to room temperature. Salt and pepper both sides and press fennel seeds into both sides of the chops. Fry the pork chops in oil in a heavy skillet over moderate to high heat.

After the chops are turned, add the garlic. Cook chops until done using caution not to burn the garlic. When the pork chops are done, remove from pan and set on warm plate. Deglaze the pan with white wine, add mushrooms, and quickly sauté. Cover pork chops with mushrooms, and serve with basmati rice and Swiss chard.

## Tia-Ginger-Chicken Sausage Pasta

Serves 4

1 medium red onion, chopped
5 large cloves garlic, crushed and chopped
1 medium jalapeño pepper, chopped and seeded
2 tablespoons olive oil
1 pound Tia-Ginger-Chicken sausage or your
    favorite uncooked sausage
6 large Crimini mushrooms or button mushrooms,
    sliced
1 can tomato sauce
½ bay leaf
½ cup red wine

Sauté the onion, garlic, and jalapeño pepper in the olive oil until fragrant. Add the sausage, either with casing removed or cut into meatball-size pieces, and sauté over medium heat until sausage is about half done. Add the mushrooms and sauté until coated with pan juices. Add the tomato sauce, bay leaf, and red wine; simmer for five to ten minutes.

   Serve over pasta or polenta.

## LOREN "SIDEKICK" FABER

Loren Faber plays harmonica with Clarence Van Hook, who nicknamed him "Sidekick." At most of my engagements, Clarence and Sidekick open the show with their folk/blues music. Sidekick offers the following recipe.

### Sonoma County Three-Bean Soup

1 ham bone
1 small onion, chopped
½ bell pepper, chopped
2 cloves garlic, chopped
Handful each: dried red kidney, Great Northern, and black beans
½ stalk of celery, chopped
Pinch of rosemary
Pinch of basil
1 carrot, cubed
1 medium potato, cubed
Elbow macaroni

Combine all ingredients except pasta in a heavy pot, cover with water, and cook over medium heat until the beans are done. Twenty minutes before beans are done, add a handful of elbow macaroni.

## LARRY JAMES

Our guitar player/vocalist Larry James has this to say about cooking: "I don't consider myself much of a cook, but I do enjoy frying up a skilletful of pork chops every now and then. My kids love 'em. This is how I prepare them."

### Larry's Pork Chops

Allow 2 chops per person

Sprinkle salt and pepper on the chops. Fry over high heat in a large, heavy cast-iron pan. When one side is brown, turn the chops over and fry with the heat turned down until well done.

When the chops are done, stir some flour into the hot grease and make a skilletful of gravy, adding salt, pepper, a dash of cayenne pepper, and some garlic salt. The gravy poured over rice and a nice lettuce and tomato salad really hits the spot!

## LUCKY OTIS

Phyllis and I have had grandson Lucky in our care since he was a little tot. That is not to say that his mom, Mercy, and his dad, Shuggie, didn't contribute to his rearing, because they certainly did. One of the pleasures in raising talented kids is watching them develop. A few years ago, Lucky said, "Hey, Grampa, how soon can I start playing in the band?" I chuckled at that because I had just bought him a bass less than a year before. The joke was on me, though, because Lucky, like his father before him, was one of those precocious youngsters who pick up music in a flash. He's been the bass player in the band for a few years now and doing a very good job.

He does a good job of eating sensibly too. His meals are vegetarian, and he knows how to combine the most mundane ingredients and make them taste great.

### Lucky's Seven-Step Pasta

1 pound noodles
1 large crown of broccoli, chopped
6 mushrooms, sliced
1 red onion, chopped
1 clove garlic, chopped
2 ounces olive oil
5 tablespoons dried basil

Boil noodles and reserve in warm water. Sauté broccoli, mushrooms, onion, and garlic in olive oil in a large, heavy-gauge skillet. Cover skillet, and simmer for 10 to 15 minutes, stirring often. Add basil to skillet, and remove from burner. Let cool 5 minutes. Combine all ingredients and enjoy a hearty, healthful dish.

## NICK OTIS

My son Nick is the drummer in my band. For over ten years, he's been the dependable backbone of our group. In addition to his solid support as a musician, he has been a positive influence on how I eat. Nicky is pretty much a complete vegetarian, and taking his advice on food has brought me to a much healthier diet.

### Nick's Millet and Peas

1 ½ cups millet
2 cups peas
½ cup almond slivers
½ cup sunflower seeds
⅛ cup soy sauce
4 celery stalks
1 cup yellow onions, chopped
1 cup mushrooms
6 cloves garlic, chopped
¼ cup olive oil
2 cups nutritional yeast
½ stick butter
Salt and pepper

Boil millet 'til almost done. Add peas, almonds, sunflower seeds, and soy sauce, and boil together 'til millet is done. Sauté celery, onions, mushrooms, and garlic in a saucepan with olive oil. Add nutritional yeast to millet while it's hot so that yeast melts in evenly. Mix in sautéed vegetables. Add butter, salt, and pepper to taste.

## Nutritional Yeast Gravy

Nondairy, no-flour gravy

Sauté together in a large saucepan: 2 stalks celery, 4 green onions, 3 cloves garlic, and 1 cup mushrooms. Stir in 3 cups of hot water and simmer until celery is soft. Add nutritional yeast, stirring constantly until you get the gravy to the consistency you prefer. Add salt and pepper to taste.

## KENDRA PARRY

"Hot Sauce Queen of Sonoma County"

Cam "Scam" Parry is my good fishing buddy and a well-known man throughout our Santa Rosa area. Many listeners know him as the character with the warped sense of humor on my weekly radio show. Less well known is his lovely wife Kenny. We call her the "hot sauce queen" because she supplies us with exotic pepper sauces. Here is a great fish recipe from Kenny.

### Baked Fish

¾ cup mayonnaise (works well with
   low-cal or no-fat mayonnaise)
1 tablespoon "hot" hot sauce (or to taste)
2 teaspoons onion, grated
2 pounds whitefish fillets
Dried bread crumbs
1½ teaspoons garlic salt
**Garnish:** 1 tablespoon parsley, finely chopped

Preheat oven to 350°. Mix mayonnaise, hot sauce, and onion. Spread on each fillet. Mix bread crumbs with garlic salt. Dip fillets in the bread crumb mixture until well coated, and place on a rack in a shallow roasting pan. Bake for 20 minutes.

## JACKIE PAYNE

Jackie Payne has been a featured vocalist in our show for almost ten years. "I'm from Georgia," he says, "and I know good cookin' when I taste it. Fried freshwater perch is a big favorite of mine. Not everyone knows how to fry fish in what I consider a proper manner. You've got to be sure the fish is cooked nice and crisp, not moist. The secret is to use a black cast-iron skillet just like the old sisters do down home, and don't try to cook too many perch in the pan at one time. It's simple, really."

### Southern-Style Fried Perch

Remove scales, head, and entrails, and wash perch thoroughly. Salt and pepper both sides liberally. Roll fish in yellow or white cornmeal. (I prefer yellow.)

Pour ½ inch of oil in skillet and heat until very hot. Add fish. When one side is fully brown and crisp, turn fish over. Do not turn the fish again. When the second side of the fish has been seared, turn down the heat, and fry until brown and crisp. Nothing to it, baby!

## DIANNE SWANN

Dianne is a vocalist in our show. We call her the "Dangerous Diva." She knows how to work an audience and have them in the palm of her hand. Here is a Dangerous Diva dish—try it, I know you'll like it

### Dangerous Diva Fish Fillets

4 medium slices of fillet of sole or
   your choice of filleted fish
1 tablespoon butter
Salt and pepper
1 teaspoon oregano
1 to 2 teaspoons garlic, minced
½ cup mushrooms, chopped
½ cup grated cheese, Monterey Jack or mozzarella
1 fresh tomato, sliced thin

Rinse fish fillets, pat dry, and dot with butter. Sprinkle fillets with salt, pepper, oregano, garlic, and mushrooms. Evenly sprinkle on cheese, and spread tomato slices over fillets. Bake in a 350° oven for approximately 30 minutes.

Serve with a tossed green salad, green beans, and garlic bread. Quick, easy, and not too dangerous for the waistline!

## NICK AND PAT VELIOTES

My brother Nick is lucky to have his wife, Patty, because while she is a fine cook, he does better as a U.S. ambassador. He has trouble boiling water!

### Cioppino

½ cup olive oil
2 yellow onions, finely chopped
3 cloves garlic, minced
2 cups canned tomato sauce
3 cups canned Italian plum tomatoes, coarsely chopped, along with the juice
1 tablespoon fresh basil, chopped
  (or 1 teaspoon dried)
1 tablespoon fresh oregano, chopped
  (or 1 teaspoon dried)
Salt and freshly ground black pepper
1 pound shrimp, shelled and de-veined
1 pound firm-fleshed whitefish fillets, cut into cubes
2 large or 4 small crabs, cleaned and cracked
12 clams, well scrubbed
½ cup parsley, minced

In a large, heavy-gauge saucepan, heat olive oil over medium heat. Sauté onions until transparent, add garlic and sauté 2 more minutes. Add tomato sauce, tomatoes, basil, oregano, and salt and pepper to taste. Bring to a boil and cook 20 minutes, stirring occasionally. Add shrimp, fish, crabs, and clams, and cook until clams open and fish is firm but tender and flakes easily (about 10 minutes).

Serve with garlic bread and a crisp green salad.

# RONALD WILSON

Ronald Wilson plays sax in my band. He is known as "The Wizard of the Reed Instruments." He plays alto, tenor, and baritone saxophone. He is also a fine clarinetist. Like many people who hail from the early era of blues/jazz music, Ronald learned how to cook. "When we were down on our luck, years ago in Chicago," he says, "I learned to make a 'poor man's stew.' As our luck improved, I actually put beef in the beef stew. You'd be surprised how good just potatoes, onions, and carrots can taste." What he offers here is a hearty beef stew with all the ingredients.

## Chicago Stew

2 packages stew meat
Flour
2 carrots, cut into 1-inch pieces
1 celery stalk, cut into ½-inch pieces
1 bell pepper, cut into ½-inch pieces
3 cloves garlic, chopped
1 can cream of celery soup
⅓ teaspoon cayenne pepper
Salt and black pepper to taste
6 or 7 potatoes, cut up

Coat meat with flour and brown in a large stewpot. Add water to cover, add all other ingredients except potatoes, and bring to a boil. Add potatoes ½ hour before meat is done.

## CARLOS ZIALCITA

Carlos Zialcita is a young blues harmonica player who resides in the San Francisco Bay Area. Originally from the Philippines, he is known as "The Thrilla from Manila." If you like country blues harp, you'll love Carlos's playing. And if you enjoy good Asian cuisine, check out this Zialcita specialty.

### Mrs. Zialcita's Chicken Adobo

3 pounds cut up chicken (I use skinless thighs
   and breasts, but you can use your favorite parts)
¾ cup white vinegar (or use whatever you have)
1½ cups light soy sauce
4 tablespoons sugar
¼ cup canola oil
10 large cloves fresh garlic, minced
Red pepper flakes or black pepper to taste
2 tablespoons fresh ginger, minced

Wash chicken, pat dry. Set aside in large bowl. Mix vinegar, soy sauce, and sugar—mixture should taste slightly salty, sweet, and tart. Set aside.

In a large pot or skillet, heat the oil. Quickly brown the chicken parts. (You're not frying the chicken; you're simply browning it). Take out the chicken and drain. In the same oil, quickly sauté the garlic and red pepper flakes. (There should be only about 3 tablespoons of oil left in the skillet.) Return the chicken to the pot. Add the vinegar, soy sauce, and sugar mixture. Stir everything around to make sure the chicken is coated. Now add the ginger. Cover and cook on top of the stove on a medium flame for about 1½ hours or until tender.

You can also bake this dish. Put the browned chicken in a casserole dish; sprinkle with the garlic, pepper flakes, and ginger and distribute evenly throughout. Pour the vinegar, soy sauce, and sugar mixture over all. Cover and bake in a 350° oven for about 1½ hours or until tender.

Serve adobo and luscious sauce over steamed rice. Delicious!

## NANCY CONZETT

No cookbook of mine would be complete without a recipe from my good friend Nancy Conzett. Nancy lives out in historic and picturesque Bodega Bay. I look forward to the days she comes into Sebastopol with a dish under her arm.

### Pear Improvisation

1 cup low-fat plain yogurt
1½ tablespoons lemon juice
1 or 2 ripe pears (Bosc are great),
   peeled and chopped
1 stalk celery, finely diced
5 or 6 dried Kalama figs, chopped
⅓ cup walnut pieces

Combine yogurt and lemon juice. Fold remaining ingredients into mixture. Allow to stand at room temperature for 15 minutes.

   Serve over a bed of mixed salad greens.

**Note:** A sprinkle of finely diced orange peel for garnish is ever so cool.

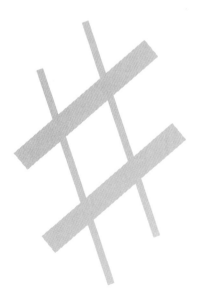

## JANICE JOHNSON

My daughter Janice is an accomplished cook and can handle many different styles of dishes. Here is one of her favorite dessert recipes.

### Homestyle Pecan Cookies

Yields 4 dozen

½ cup brown sugar
½ cup granulated sugar
½ cup butter, softened
1 egg
¾ teaspoon vanilla extract
1⅛ cups sifted flour
½ teaspoon salt
½ cup pecan pieces

In a bowl, combine sugar and butter thoroughly. Add egg and vanilla. In another bowl, combine flour and salt. Blend in butter and egg mixture and add nuts. With a teaspoon, drop spoonfuls of mixture 2 inches apart on greased cookie sheets. Bake at 350° for 10 to 12 minutes until brown. Let stand 5 minutes. With a greased spatula, remove cookies carefully.

## HELEN KRONICK

Helen and her husband, Hal, are longtime good friends to Phyllis and me. Through the years, we've enjoyed Helen's tasty cooking a lot. Every year, I make sure to send Helen some Gravenstein apples from our orchard. When I do, I know Helen will make us an apple pie as only she can make it.

### Apple Pie

**Crust:**
2 cups flour
½ teaspoon salt
¾ cup shortening (Crisco)
3 tablespoons ice water

Sift together flour and salt. Work shortening into the flour with pastry blender until grain in the mixture is about pea size. Stir in ice water, 1 tablespoon at a time, until the mixture holds together. Divide in half, and roll out between two pieces of wax paper.

**Filling:**
⅓ cup white sugar
⅓ cup light brown sugar
2 tablespoons cornstarch
¼ teaspoon cinnamon
⅛ teaspoon nutmeg
4 to 5 cups apples, diced
1½ tablespoons butter

Mix together dry ingredients and sift over apples until well coated. Line pie pan with crust and filling, and dot with butter. Cover with top crust.

Bake in 450° oven for 10 minutes. Reduce heat to 350° and bake until done, about 1 hour in all.

## ELMER LEE THOMAS

Elmer Lee Thomas is the leader of a popular acoustic blues bland. Acoustic instrumental groups are very rare in this era of electrified bands, and it is a pleasure to hear the young men and women in Elmer Lee's band play the early blues selection in such an authentic manner.

### Deluxe Baked Cheesecake

¾ cup butter or margarine, softened
1¼ cups plus 3 tablespoons flour
3 egg yolks
Grated peel of 3 lemons
5 8-ounce packages of cream cheese
1¾ cups sugar
5 eggs
¼ cup heavy whipping cream
1 tablespoon grated orange peel
¼ teaspoon salt
**Garnish:** 1 cup sour cream

In small bowl with mixer at low speed, beat butter, 1¼ cups flour, 1 egg yolk, and half of lemon peel until dough is well mixed. Refrigerate, covered, for 1 hour.

Preheat oven to 400°, press ⅓ of dough into bottom of 10-inch springform pan. Bake 8 minutes. Allow to cool.

Turn oven to 475°. In large bowl with mixer at medium speed, beat cream cheese until smooth. Slowly beat in 1¾ cups sugar until smooth.

With mixer at low speed, beat in 3 tablespoons flour and remaining ingredients. Beat 5 minutes at high speed.

Press rest of dough around sides of springform pan to within 1 inch of top. (Do not bake dough.)

Pour cheese mixture into pan. Bake 12 minutes. Turn oven to 300° and bake 35 minutes. Turn oven off; leave cake in oven for 30 minutes. Cool on rack in pan, then chill well.

**To serve:** Remove sides of pan, loosen cake from bottom with large spatula and slide onto serving plate. Spread top of cheesecake with sour cream.

## Old-Fashioned Tea Cakes

3½ cups all-purpose flour
2 cups sugar
2½ sticks (1¼ cups) butter
2 eggs
2½ teaspoons double-acting baking powder
2 tablespoons milk
1 teaspoon brandy (or to taste)
½ teaspoon salt

Measure ingredients into large bowl. With mixer set to medium speed, beat until well mixed, occasionally scraping bowl. Shape dough into two balls. Wrap in wax paper and refrigerate 2 to 3 hours, until easy to handle.

On lightly floured surface, roll out one-half of dough to ¼ inch thick for crisp cookies. With floured cookie cutter, cut into shapes.

Place cookies ½ inch apart on cookie sheet. Bake at 400° for 8 minutes, until very light brown. With pancake turner, transfer cookies to a rack to cool.

## CLARENCE VAN HOOK

Back in the 1960s, Clarence was quite popular as a singer/guitarist in the coffeehouse and folk club scene, but he had other ideas. He told me, "This is great fun, but I like to eat three meals a day and my wife and kids have the same habit, so I'm gonna get me an electrical contractor's license and the music can be a pleasant sideline." His business, Van Hook Electric, is located in Richmond, California.

We hooked up together again after I moved back to northern California in 1990. Since then, we've worked together a lot. In fact, he is the opening act at my regular Saturday night gig at the Blues and Boogie Room of the Fun House Club in Santa Rosa.

The following recipe is one of Clarence's favorites. I've always thought Old-Time Nut Cake was quite an appropriate recipe for Clarence. But he ain't that nutty—he still says, "Music is fun, but I'm not quittin' my day job!"

### Old-Time Nut Cake

2¾ cups sifted cake flour
2 teaspoons baking powder
1 teaspoon salt
1 cup (2 sticks) butter or margarine
1¾ cups sugar
4 eggs
⅔ cup milk
2 teaspoons vanilla
1 cup very finely chopped nuts (use hickory nuts, black walnuts or pecans)

Grease a 9-inch tube pan and dust lightly with flour.

Sift flour, baking powder, and salt into wax paper; reserve. Beat butter or margarine, sugar, and eggs in large bowl of mixer at high speed for 3 minutes. Remove bowl from mixer. Stir in dry ingredients alternating with milk, beating after each addition until batter is smooth. Stir in vanilla and nuts.

Pour batter into prepared pan. Bake in moderate oven at 350° for 1 hour and 5 minutes or until center springs back when lightly pressed with fingertip. Cool in pan on wire rack 10 minutes. Loosen cake around tube and outside edge with a knife, and turn out onto wire rack; cool completely. Frost top and sides.

## CHARLES WILLIAMS

In 1980, during my eleven-year tenure as pastor of the Landmark Church in Los Angeles, I noticed that a young kid in my church choir was a sensational gospel singer. Years later, I moved him into my R&B revue, and he developed into an exciting performer. We did a number of recordings together. The albums Charles was featured on include *Otisology; Johnny Otis; Johnny Otis, Through the 80s;* and *The New Johnny Otis Show.* Today, Charles leads his own Charles Williams Revue based in San Jose, California.

In addition to his talent as a moving gospel-tinged singer, Charles is a very accomplished cook. Here are two examples of Charles's culinary ability.

### Easy Sour Cream Pound Cake

1 cup (2 sticks) butter or margarine
3 cups sugar
6 eggs
3 cups flour
¼ teaspoon baking soda
Less than ¼ teaspoon salt
1 cup sour cream
1 teaspoon vanilla

Cream together butter sugar. Add eggs. Mix flour and other dry ingredients together. Add to creamed butter and sugar alternating with sour cream. Add vanilla.

Pour into greased tube pan. Bake approximately 2 hours in 225° oven. Cool. Eat plain, or add your choice of frosting and sprinkle with chopped nuts, if desired.

## Vanilla Wafer Cake

1 cup (2 sticks) butter
1 cup sugar
6 eggs
12 ounces crushed vanilla wafers
½ cup milk
1 cup chopped pecans or walnuts
1 7-ounce package shredded coconut

Cream butter thoroughly. Add sugar gradually, 'til light and fluffy. Add eggs, one at a time; beat well. Fold in vanilla wafers, milk, nuts, and coconut. Pour into bundt or tube pan that has been greased and floured. Bake at 300° for 1½ hours. Cool in pan for 20 minutes, then remove.

# METRIC CONVERSION TABLE

## LIQUID MEASURES

| U.S. Measures | Fluid Ounces | Imperial Measures | Milliliters |
|---|---|---|---|
| 1 teaspoon | ⅛ | 1 teaspoon | 5 |
| 2 teaspoons | ¼ | 1 dessertspoon | 10 |
| 1 tablespoon | ½ | 1 tablespoon | 15 |
| 2 tablespoons | 1 | 2 tablespoons | 30 |
| ¼ cup | 2 | 4 tablespoons | 56 |
| ⅓ cup | 2⅔ | | 80 |
| ½ cup | 4 | | 110 |
| ⅔ cup | 5 | ¼ pint / 1 gill | 140 |
| ¾ cup | 6 | | 170 |
| 1 cup / ½ pint | 8 | | 225 |
| 1¼ cups | 10 | ½ pint | 280 |
| 1½ cups | 12 | | 420 |
| 2 cups / 1 pint | 16 | generous ¾ pint | 450 |
| 2½ cups | 20 | 1 pint | 560 |
| 3 cups / 1½ pints | 24 | | 675 |
| 3½ cups | 27 | | 750 |
| 3¾ cups | 30 | 1½ pints | 840 |
| 4 cups / 2 pints / 1 quart | 32 | | 900 |
| 4½ cups | 36 | | 1000 / 1 liter |
| 5 cups | 40 | | 1120 |
| 6 cups / 3 pints | 48 | scant 2½ pints | 1350 |
| 7 cups | 56 | 2¾ pints | 1600 |
| 8 cups / 2 quarts | 64 | 3¼ pints | 1800 |
| 9 cups | 72 | 3½ pints | 2000 / 2 liters |
| 10 cups / 5 pints | 80 | 4 pints | 2250 |

## SOLID MEASURES

| U.S. and Imperial | Metric Equivalent | U.S. and Imperial | Metric Equivalent |
|---|---|---|---|
| 1 oz. | 25 g. | 12 oz. / ¾ lb. | 350 g. |
| 1½ oz. | 40 g. | 16 oz. / 1 lb. | 450 g. |
| 2 oz. | 50 g. | 1¼ lb. | 575 g. |
| 3 oz. | 60 g. | 1½ lb. | 675 g. |
| 3½ oz. | 100 g. | 1¾ lb. | 800 g. |
| 4 oz. / ¼ lb. | 110 g. | 2 lb. | 900 g. |
| 5 oz. | 150 g. | 2¼ lb. | 1000 / 1 kg. |
| 6 oz. | 175 g. | 3 lb. | 1 kg. 350 g. |
| 7 oz. | 200 g. | 4 lb. | 1 kg. 800 g. |
| 8 oz. / ½ lb. | 225 g. | 4½ lb. | 2 kg. |
| 9 oz. | 250 g. | 5 lb. | 2 kg. 250 g. |
| 10 oz. | 275 g. | 6 lb. | 2 kg. 750 g. |

## OVEN TEMPERATURES

| Fahrenheit | Celsius | Gas Mark | Heat of Oven |
|---|---|---|---|
| 225° | 110° | ¼ | Very cool |
| 250° | 120° | ½ | Very cool |
| 275° | 140° | 1 | Cool |
| 300° | 150° | 2 | Cool |
| 325° | 160° | 3 | Moderate |
| 350° | 180° | 4 | Moderate |
| 375° | 190° | 5 | Moderately hot |
| 400° | 200° | 6 | Moderately hot |
| 425° | 220° | 7 | Hot |
| 450° | 230° | 8 | Hot |
| 475° | 240° | 9 | Very hot |